Unto the Thousandth Generation

Unto the Thousandth Generation

The Evangelical Importance of an Eschatology that Embraces Suffering for Christ

Paul D. LeFavor

Blacksmith Publishing

Fayetteville, North Carolina 28304

Unto the Thousandth Generation:
The Evangelical Importance of an Eschatology that
Embraces Suffering for Christ
by Paul D. LeFavor

Copyright © 2017 by Blacksmith LLC

Library of Congress Number: 2017964693

ISBN 978-0-9977434-3-2

Printed in the United States of America

Published by Blacksmith LLC
Fayetteville, NC

www.Blacksmithpublishing .com

Direct inquiries and/or orders to the above web address.

To Becky,
a most rare jewel.

"Wrath brings the punishment of the sword, but those who survived the sword found grace in the wilderness (Gen 3:24; Job 19:24; Jer 31:2; Mt 10:34; Rev 1:16; 6:2; 19:11-21)."

Contents

Preface

"By eternal covenant's confirmation; Steadfast love unto the thousandth generation."

Contrary to popular belief, eschatology drives, or at least affects in large measure, one's evangelical beliefs and efforts. For example, millions of professing Christians believe in a rapture which envisions an escape from tribulation. They ask: How could God allow His Church to suffer? Such thinking leaves God's people unprepared for trials and, for the most part, socially irresponsible. However, Christ tells us to expect tribulation (Jn 16:33) and even rejoice in it (Mt 5:12; cf. 1 Pet 4:12)! As we will argue, a resurrection will occur at Christ's second coming, in which all the dead will be raised up. This resurrection will coincide with the return of Christ and the end of the world, and will precede the final judgement (2 Thess 1:7-10). Another prominent error in the Church, which correlates to and is driven by rapture theology, presents us with a separate saving program for the ethnic nation of Israel, leading many Christians, in large measure, to fall short in their evangelistic efforts to Jews.

The purpose of this study is threefold: First, to confront issues like these with biblical truth and demonstrate from biblical studies, Church history and systematic theology that the phrase "Great Tribulation" is a technical term referring to the end time trial which has already been set in motion by Christ's first advent and will culminate with His second advent (Acts 14:22; 1 Cor 11:25; Rev 7:14); second, to argue that God has a providential purpose for tribulation to be a means for:

(1) the purification of the Church (2 Cor 1:3-9); (2) the gathering of the elect (Col 1:24); and (3) the talionic judgment of the reprobate (Mt 25:31-46); and third, to demonstrate the manner in which John's 'tribulation-kingdom-endurance' triad in Rev 1:9 forms a paradigmatic structure in the Apocalypse, Christ's end times discourses in the gospels as well as the Pauline corpus.

My agenda will be to gain a thorough understanding of tribulation. Beginning with definitions, my method will be to explore the various words associated with it, and make certain distinctions between it and the wrath of God. This will be the focus of chapter one. In chapters two and three, I will move to survey what the whole Bible has to teach us regarding tribulation and God's purpose for it. Then in chapter four I will explore what the church has believed regarding tribulation, and in chapters five through seven, end with some practical applications from all that will be surveyed.

The goal of this study is to persuade believers to adopt an eschatology that embraces suffering for Christ. A right understanding of this is crucial for the Church to fulfill the Great Commission (Mt 24:14).

Paul D. LeFavor
Reformation Day
October 31, 2017
500 Years of
Reformation

Chapter One:
God's Purpose for Tribulation

"Beloved, do not be surprised at the fiery trial when it comes upon you to test you, as though something strange were happening to you. But rejoice insofar as you share Christ's sufferings, that you may also rejoice and be glad when his glory is revealed" (1 Peter 4:12-13).

The prevalent eschatological view in the evangelical church today is one that envisions Christ's second coming in two stages.[1] First, a rapture for the church when believers will be caught up to meet the Lord in the air, remain with Him in heaven for a seven-year period while the great tribulation is going on, and afterward return with Christ to the earth as He brings judgment. This view is known as pretribulationism because it believes Christ will remove the church before the tribulation. Despite the popularity of this end-time view, due in large measure by the notes in Scofield's Reference Bible, it is as unbiblical as it is impractical.[2]

Over against this view, my intent will be to argue that the church, as brothers and fellow partakers of Christ's kingdom, must continue to endure tribulation, while faithfully testifying the gospel, until all Israel is saved and then the end will come (Mt 24:14; Jn 16:33; Rom 11:26). Christ gave His church

---

[1] Tim F. LaHaye, *No Fear of the Storm* (Sisters, OR: Multnomah, 1992), 23-38.
[2] The Cyrus I. Scofield Reference Bible (1909) has single-handedly made the dispensational pretribulational end-time scheme by far the most popular in the United States with sales in the tens of millions.

teaching on tribulation because His intent was for the church to not only survive all tribulation, including the "Great Tribulation," but to conquer through it. Despite the biblical warrant for this view, the majority of Evangelical Christians today are adamant that a pretribulation rapture will remove them from any such trouble under the assumption that Christ would never allow His bride to go through such suffering.

Voicing the prominent eschatological perspective of today, Tim LaHaye passionately declares, "Plainly, if the church were to go through the tribulation, she would not survive it."[3] Yet, does the Bible really teach that Christians will be removed from tribulation and suffering? My goal is to present a biblical argument that demonstrates that tribulation is the cost for winning the lost, as the sufferings of believers extend Christ's afflictions to the people they were meant to save (Is 53:10-11; 2 Cor 1:6; Col 1:24).

I will demonstrate this from the Word of God and Christian history, arguing that tribulation fulfils God's purpose by (1) purifying and strengthening His church, (2) affording His saints an opportunity to testify to the effectual gathering of all the elect, and (3) serving as the means for hardening and judging the reprobate. By advancing this argument, I will show the evangelical importance of having an eschatology that embraces suffering for Christ.

---

[3] Tim F. LaHaye, *Rapture Under Attack: Will You Escape the Tribulation?* (Sisters, OR: Multnomah, 1998), 62.

To narrow our focus, it is not our intent to enter the debate regarding the thousand years of Revelation 20 in an effort to argue for either a premillennial, amillennial or postmillennial view. While I hold to an amillennial view, it seems where one would place the millennium is irrespective, granted that a Dispensational perspective is not employed. [4] For in all non-Dispensational millennial views, the church endures all tribulation before the return of Christ; albeit in the power of Christ.[5] With the question of the millennium aside, though I will need to interact a little with it further, it is fair to say that while a great many Christians today don't hold to a fully-orbed Dispensationalism, they have adopted its end time scheme.[6]

---

[4] Dispensationalism is a school of thought within Christianity that sees God in the Bible as structuring His relationship with mankind along stewardships or 'dispensations.'

[5] There is another variety of eschatology known as the mid-tribulational view, but it seems that those who hold to it are also dispensationalists.

[6] Amillennial and Postmillennial views understand the millennium of Revelation 20:1-6 to be the interadvent period; with a further differentiation being, in the Amill position Christ's reign began with His incarnation, ministry, crucifixion, and intercession, etc. while Postmills, differing about the timing of the binding of Satan, see the binding as some future event, an event that will eventually lead to a global Christian world. However, many Postmills place the binding at the first advent, and thus have little difference with many Amills. Over against this, the second view lines up with what is called the Historic Premill and Dispensational view which understands the millennium to occur after Christ's second advent. Further, it must be stated that while those of the second viewpoint share their understanding of when the millennial reign occurs, they differ in their view of the saving program of God: Dispensational Premills hold that there are two distinct peoples of God – Israel and the church, and that the 1000

While tribulation covers all aspects of anti-covenantal trouble God's people encounter, from Abel to the return of Christ, the term "Great Tribulation" refers to the duration of history between Christ's first and second advents. Adding a further distinction, it may be said with a good degree of exegetical certainty that this great tribulation "will be intensified in its severity toward the end of history."[7] However, many Christians believe that the church will not survive the tribulation. Why? The answer seems to be that they misunderstand the differences between the wrath of God and tribulation. With this issue cleared up, gaining a biblical understanding of God's purpose for tribulation is bound to occur. To clarify this distinction, my method will be to outline the concept of tribulation in terms of definition, duration and design.

The Definition of Tribulation

As the Bible declares, the world stands under the wrath of God (Jn 3:36). Accordingly, suffering is part and parcel of living in a fallen world. In light of this troublesome fact, Thomas à Kempis advises, "so long as we continue in this world, we must not flatter ourselves with an imagination so vain as that of being exempted from tribulations and trials." Moreover, death itself is proof of the ongoing wrath of God (Gen 3:15-24; Rom 5:12-21; 8:18-20). Thus, in addition to the "thousand natural shocks that flesh is heir to," tribulation is pressure which causes distress and

---

year reign of Christ on earth is with Israel, not the church while Historic Premills do not.

[7] Greg K. Beale, *The Book of Revelation* (Grand Rapids, MI: Eerdmans, 1999), 434.

affliction taking on various mental, emotional, physical, or spiritual forms.

The word 'tribulation' in the Greek is *thlipsis* θλῖψις from *thlibo* θλίβω, means 'to press' or 'to hem in,' and often serves to translate צֵרתי *tsar* in the LXX (cf. Ps 46:1).[8] And in our English Bible, there are a host of words associated with tribulation such as: crush, press together, squash, hem in, compress, shake violently or squeeze. Additionally, tribulation may vary from false teaching to overt oppression (Rev 2:9, 20).

Sometimes it is economically oriented and may include legal action by the state against the church to include imprisonment and death (Acts 16:20-24; Heb 10:34). But whatever form tribulation takes, it is always brought on the people of God for their faithfulness. The picture one gets from the word "tribulation" is that of a believer who is facing situations in which they are, as it were, between a rock and a hard place, being 'hemmed in' with only one way to go (Acts 13:50).

Respectively, the basis for tribulation may be said to be covenant loyalty. This is because the two basic forms tribulation can take on interact with the covenant: (1) First, tribulation, in the form of persecution, arises on account of the worship of God,

---

[8] Θλῖψις and θλίβω which is normally translated 'tribulation,' 'affliction,' 'distress' or 'trouble,' is used a total of 55 times in the New Testament and indicates being crowded, afflicted, distressed, and caused to suffer (Mt 7:14; 13:21; 24:9; 24:21, 29, 31; Mk 3:9; 4:17; 13:19, 24; Jn 16:21, 33; Acts 7:10, 11, 19; 14:22; 20:23; Rom 2:9; 5:3 (x2); 8:35; 12:12; 1 Cor 7:28; 2 Cor 1:4 (x2); 1:6, 8; 2:4; 4:8, 17; 6:4; 7:4, 5; 8:2, 13; Eph 3:13; Phil 1:16, 17; 4:14; Col 1:24; 1 Thess 3:3, 4, 7; 2 Thess 1:4, 6 (x2), 7; 1 Tim 5:10; Heb 10:33; 11:37; Jas 1:27; Rev 1:9; 2:9, 10, 22; 7:14).

the gospel message, and holy living (Rev 12:11; 14:6).[9] For believers, tribulation in this sense comes in the form of a trial in order to test and refine faith. Moreover, in persecution, (as is quite often overlooked) tribulation may take on a redemptive function, actuating the remnant (Acts 8:1; 14:19-28; 2 Cor 1:6; Col 1:24).

Second, tribulation takes the form of divine wrath and punishment for unbelievers (2 Thess 1:6). The Bible declares that in this second form of tribulation, God may employ various agents (malevolent or benevolent), to carry out His purposes (Ex 12:12, 23; Lk 21:23).[10] The nature of this form of tribulation is described by the Bible's own terms to be: wrath (Zeph 1:15); punishment (Is 24:21); destruction (Dan 9:27); an overflowing scourge (Is 28:15); and vengeance (Is 35:4; 61:2).

An objection often raised for what has just been articulated is this: Tribulation is the eschatological period of divine judgment that precedes the time of Israel's national conversion and Christ's establishment of His kingdom on earth.[11] However, as it will be discovered, this objection is grown out a dogmatic bias that unbiblically separates Israel from the church as well as a misunderstanding of the nature of Christ's kingdom.

---

[9] In Rev 14:6, the gospel is said to be eternal. Therefore, the OT saints can be said to have been persecuted for the gospel's sake (cf. Mt 23:35).

[10] Compare Exodus 12:12 with Exodus 12:23.

[11] Thomas Ice and Timothy J. Demy, *The Return: Understanding Christ's Second Coming and the End Times* (Grand Rapids, MI: Kregel, 1999), 28.

If the above can be clarified, and if it can be demonstrated that there are differences between divine wrath and tribulation, then the issue should be settled, and we should all agree that God has a purpose for the church to be in tribulation. For the present let it be said that behind the first form of tribulation lies the demonic rage of Satan as it is directed through the instrumentality of the unbelieving world toward God, His covenant, and His covenant bearers (Gal 4:29; Rev 13:6). An important consideration is, while the first form of tribulation is satanically inspired and may be used by God to chasten and discipline His adopted sons and daughters, the second form, as will be argued, is only for unbelievers as it is divine wrath on account of God's retributive justice. Regardless of which form tribulation may take, it is controlled by the One who sits upon the throne (Rev 6:1).[12] Ultimately, as will be argued, tribulation is God's means of effecting separation and making a distinction between His people and the unbelieving world (Ex 8:23; Hag 2:6-7; Mt 10:34; Acts 14:22).

Moreover, we are reminded that Christ is sovereign and has all authority in heaven and earth and under the earth (Phil 2:10). This is a cause for much peace in affliction. For believers may take heart that all suffering is for God's glory and our good (Rom 8:28). This is the impression one gets when hearing truths such as:

---

[12] William Hendriksen, *More Than Conquerors: An Interpretation of the Book of Revelation* (Grand Rapids, MI: Baker, 2002), 113.

We are afflicted Θλιβόμενοι[13] in every way, but not crushed; perplexed; but not driven to despair; persecuted, but not forsaken; struck down, but not destroyed" (2 Cor 4:8-9); and "they will deliver you up to tribulation θλῖψιν and put you to death, and you will be hated by all nations for my name's sake. But the one who endures to the end will be saved" (Mt 24:9, 13);[14] and "If we are afflicted θλιβόμεθα, it is for your comfort and salvation" (2 Cor 1:6).[15]

Looking back at these scriptures, the first text (2 Cor 4:8-9) provides us with a definition for tribulation as well as a range of what may be expected for being a believer in a world that hates Christ (cf. Jn 15:18-25). As the definition suggests, tribulations come upon Christ by way of His followers (Jn 16:33; Col 1:24; 2 Tim 3:12). The second text (Mt 24:9, 13) enables us to understand that tribulation will end only with Christ's second advent (2 Thess 1:6-7; Rev 12:13-17). Though it remains to be demonstrated, it may be said that "the great tribulation has been inaugurated with Jesus and the church."[16] In the preterist scheme, however, the great tribulation has already occurred with the leveling

---

[13] Θλίβω here is used in the present passive participial form which conveys the idea of the continuous nature of tribulation and distress. Thus tribulation is a present reality.

[14] The end in view in verse 13 is to be understood as the end of history either personally (with the believer's death) or at Christ's Second Coming, whichever comes first.

[15] Θλίβω is used here in the present indicative passive tense indicating that pressures and afflictions come upon believers for the sake of Christ as in Luke 22:28-29. This aspect will be covered more in chapter 1.

[16] Greg K. Beale, *New Testament Biblical Theology: The Unfolding of the Old Testament in the New* (Grand Rapids, MI: Baker, 2011), 218.

of Jerusalem and the destruction of the temple. In passing, let it be said that this understanding fails to account for how tribulation will affect the churches of Asia Minor and the whole earth (Rev 12:9; 16:14). Finally, the third text (2 Cor 1:6) enables us to envision God's redemptive purpose for tribulation.

What remains to be seen in our argument above is the manner in which God preserves believers safely in the hands of Christ despite tribulation (Jn 10:28-29). For now, let me summarize by saying: As persecution from an unbelieving world is meant for evil, God ordains it for His glory and the good of His church (Gen 50:19-20; Rom 8:28). What's more, tribulation is not only part and parcel of the saints anticipated earthly sojourn, it also serves to wield and temper Christ's corporate body into an effective instrument for emancipating the lost (Jn 16:33). We now turn to define wrath and by so doing differentiate it with tribulation.

The Definition of Wrath

The word 'wrath' in the Greek *orgeh* ὀργή is used 36 times in the New Testament (NT) and can mean 'anger,' 'wrath,' 'passion,' or 'vengeance,' and apart from two instances, it always refers to the wrath of God (Eph 4:31; Col 3:8). Similarly, the word *orgizo* ὀργίζω, meaning to be angry or enraged, is used eight times referring to divine anger as well as human and demonic rage (Lk 14:21; 15:28). The differences between the two words may be seen in Revelation 11:18 which declares: "The nations raged (ὀργίζω), but Your [God's] wrath (ὀργή) came."

9

What's the difference? Whereas God's wrath is completely righteous in character, mankind's is not. From this we can make three biblical observations: (1) God's wrath is directed against all ungodliness and unrighteousness of men (Rom 1:18; 3:10). As John Murray observes, "Wrath is the holy revulsion of God's being against that which is the contradiction of his holiness;"[17] (2) God's wrath is ongoing (Jn 3:36). As George Ladd observes: "God's judgments against evil have been operating throughout the course of human history."[18] And (3) God's wrath is His warning to mankind (Rev 9:20). As we stated earlier, death itself is a warning.

The point is believers are saved in Christ from God's ongoing wrath which will also manifest itself in a future out-pouring at the time of the end (1 Thess 1:10; cf. Jn 3:36). There yet remains a future final judgment where everyone who is not included in Christ will suffer an eternal punishment (Acts 17:31; Rev 20:11-15). Thus, while believers may not know precisely why they are suffering, they can rest assured that they will never suffer God's wrath – Christ has already done that for them (Jn 3:16, 35; Rom 3:25). However, though delivered from God's wrath, believers may displease the Lord, and provoking Him to anger, may incur His fatherly chastisement (Heb 12:7-11).

Digging deeper, if asked: "What is the basis for God's wrath?" When surveying the Bible, God's wrath begins with man's failure in Eden, when, upon the sin of our first parents, God unsheathed the sword, pronounced

---

[17] John Murray, *The Epistle to the Romans* (Grand Rapids, MI: Eerdmans, 1959), 35.
[18] George Ladd, *The Blessed Hope* (Grand Rapids, MI: Eerdmans, 1956), 124.

the sentence of death upon all them (and all mankind), and drove them out of paradise (Gen 3:24; cf. Rom 5:12).[19] The only entrance back into the paradise of God is now barred in the "narrow way" with a flaming sword (Gen 3:24; Mt 7:14). But in the fullness of time, by the unmerited favor of God, Christ the Redeemer suffered the vengeance of the covenant on behalf of His own, forever absorbing the wrath of God due them, and made a way for them back into paradise.

According to the Bible, everyone belongs to one of either two covenants – that of Adam and the covenant of works (Rom 5:12; cf. Jn 3:34; Rom 1:18; 5:12), or of Christ, the second Adam, and the covenant of grace (Gen 15: Ps 50:5; Rom 5:15-21). For those under the covenant of works "the wrath of God remains upon them" (Jn 3:36), such as may be felt, as a "sense of God's revenging wrath, horror of conscience, and a fearful expectation of judgment, are to the wicked the beginning of their torments which they shall endure after death" (Shorter Catechism 83). Moreover, in Christ, the elect "survive the sword" and find "grace in the wilderness" (Jer 31:2; Rev 12:14); the wilderness (desert) itself being both a place of persecution as well as preservation (Rev 12:14).

These two concepts of tribulation and wrath come together in Paul's First Epistle to the Thessalonians when he writes that the church has not been appointed for "wrath" (1 Thess 1:10) but for "tribulation" (1 Thess 3:3-4). Not only that, it is the suffering of tribulation in fact that leads Paul to say that the church in

---

[19] For clarification, it seems that the Old Testament "vengeance of the covenant" is a technical term relating to divine wrath which God directs against apostates along with the unbelieving world (Lev 26:25; Lk 18:15).

Thessalonica is shown to be elect (2 Thess 1:5-6). In other words, the Thessalonian believer's partaking of Christ's tribulations (θλίψεων) is proof of their election. The point is, God makes a distinction between His own people and an unbelieving world (Ex 11:7). Something Paul also teaches us in this passage is the present tribulation which began with Christ's first coming will end only with His second coming (2 Thess 1:7-8).

The Duration of Tribulation

While pretribulationists correctly affirm that the great tribulation will occur prior to and end with Christ's second coming, they wrongly insist that this period comes only after the rapture of the church.[20] Pretribulationists wrongly view the great tribulation as a future seven-year period in which God's wrath is poured out on the earth. However, as we've stated, the Bible declares God's wrath as ongoing (Jn 3:36; Rom 1:18). In light of what the Scripture teaches, a seven-year period of tribulation is a dubious teaching.

Central to this debate, Dispensationalists claim that Daniel 9:24-27 presents a seven-year period of tribulation in which the Antichrist will afflict the world along with God's people, whom the Dispensationalists believe to be ethnic Jews.[21] Our treatment of Daniel 9:24-27 will be dealt with in chapter two, but suffice it to say that the period in question in Daniel 7:25; 9:27; and 12:7, corresponds to the duration of time between

---

[20] Lewis S. Chafer and John F. Walvoord, *Major Bible Themes* (Grand Rapids, MI: Zondervan, 1974), 322.
[21] Walvoord, *Major Bible Themes*, 316-318.

Christ's first and second advents. The point is, the great tribulation, which corresponds to this present age, is also the end times (Heb 1:2). Thus, this present time period will consummate only with the last trumpet which also announces the end of the world and the coming general resurrection (Jn 5:28-29; Rev 20:11-15).

The Design of Tribulation

I am arguing that God's purpose for the church is to remain steadfast throughout all tribulation until the end comes. Can it therefore be argued that there is a purpose or design for this? Let it first be said that tribulation begins the moment the new life is given. Summoning His own, Christ declares "Enter by the narrow gate....For the gate is narrow and the way is hard τεθλιμμένη (θλίβω) that leads to life, and those who find it are few" (Mt 7:14).[22] Thus, "through many tribulations we must enter the kingdom of God" (Acts 14:22). The point is, the Scriptures declare that God has a providential purpose for all tribulation, and no sooner do believers experience the new life in Christ than they experience the world's hatred for their Master (Jn 15:18).

As stated earlier, tribulation sovereignly fulfills God's purpose by: (1) purifying and strengthening His church, (2) affording His saints an opportunity to testify unto the effectual gathering of all the elect, as well as (3) serving as the means for hardening and judging the reprobate. Under our first point, it may be

---

[22] Mattill, Andrew J., "The Way of Tribulation," *Journal of Biblical Literature* 98 (1979): 531-546.

said that God ordains suffering to purify and strengthen believers by separating them from the false contentment of the world, so that they will rely more on the Lord and not on themselves (2 Cor 1:9; 12:9; 1 Pet 5:6-7). In this way, suffering is a means for God to sanctify believers, forging Christ's character in them (Ps 119:66-67, 71; Pro 27:17; Rom 5:1-5; Heb 2:10; 5:8). Moreover, God employs suffering as a means of disciplining us so that we will avoid future opportunities to sin; God scourges every son He receives (Heb 12:6).

As to our second point, we may say that God uses suffering to create in us staying power to faithfully endure persecution (Jam 1:2-8). In this way God prepares His saints for trouble by causing them to experience suffering.[23] It is suffering therefore that not only affords Christians the opportunity to witness the saving power of Christ (2 Cor 4:10-11; Col 1:24-29; 1 Pet 2:19-20), but moreover affords God the opportunity to manifest His grace. Suffering is thus the price for winning the lost for Christ, to fulfill the Great Commission (Mt 24:9-14; 28:18-20).

Over against what has been articulated here, many Christians believe physical sufferings are not to be the experience of the church.[24] In light of speculations such as these, a question one might ask is: "How does physical suffering fit into God's scheme of things?" According to Kenneth Copeland, it belongs exclusively

---

[23] However, this is not just for sufferings sake, but because God's wisdom is as manifold as it is infinite, He causes us to grow in grace, mirroring Christ's image, thereby creating staying power in us, while He prunes us of our sinful proclivities (Jn 15:1-8).
[24] Ice, *The Return*, 28.

on the cross. Under the heading 'What about suffering with Christ?' he states:

> The only suffering we encounter in sharing his (Christ's) victory is spiritual. That's what the Word is talking about when it says we are to be partakers of Christ's suffering. In other words, the only suffering for a believer is the spiritual discomfort brought by resisting the pressures of the flesh, not a physical or mental suffering.[25]

The Word of God on the other hand, teaches us that suffering is not the exception but the expectation of the church as Jesus said "In the world you will have tribulation" (Jn 16:33). Jesus commands His own to prepare themselves mentally; "they will deliver you up to tribulation θλῖψις and put you to death, and you will be hated by all nations for my name's sake" (Mt 24:9).

Looking to our third point, tribulation serves as the means for hardening and judging the reprobate. This argument will be developed in later chapters, however, in passing, let it be said that unbelievers, duped by Satan, are the unwitting instruments of tribulation as it is directed against the people of God (2 Cor 4:4). And as the reprobate, seeking to rid themselves of those who bring the offending message, persecute the saints, as Edmund Clowney observes, "the sword of judgment is drawn on behalf of God's people."[26]

---

[25] Kenneth Copeland, "What about Suffering with Christ?" available from http://www.kcm.org/index.php?p=real_help_content&id=1371; Internet; accessed 03 June 2016.

[26] Edmund P. Clowney, *The Unfolding Mystery: Discovering Christ in the Old Testament* (Phillipsburg, NJ: P&R, 2013), 12.

Thus, as believers, we may not know precisely why we are suffering, but in Christ, we can be assured that all of our sufferings are for the glory of God and our good (Rom 8:28). Ultimately, suffering sovereignly fulfills God's purpose by purifying and strengthening those who repent and believe the gospel while the reprobate are hardened and judged. We now move to examine the Old Testament's teaching on tribulation.

Chapter Two:
Tribulation in the Old Testament

"So He humbled you, allowed you to hunger, and fed you with manna which you did not know nor did your fathers know, that He might make you know that man shall not live by bread alone; but man lives by every word that proceeds from the mouth of the Lord" (Dt 8:3).

As Edmund Clowney put it, "The Bible has a story line. It traces an unfolding drama." [27] Our challenge is to trace the manner in which tribulation interacts with the Bible's overall story line. Beginning with the Old Testament (OT), our method will be to frame our discussion with our three propositions introduced in chapter one: tribulation sovereignly fulfills God's purpose by: (1) gathering the elect (by effecting separation), (2) purifying and strengthening the elect, as well as (3) serving as the means for hardening and judging the reprobate.

Covenant-Kingdom and the Inaugurated End-Times

As we move to consider the OT's teaching regarding tribulation, as stated earlier, for many Christians, tribulation is merely the eschatological period of divine judgment at the end of history which precedes the time of Israel's national conversion as well as the establishment of Christ's kingdom on earth. However, as Robert Gundry points out, misunderstandings such as these "rest on insufficient

---

[27] Edmund P. Clowney, *The Unfolding Mystery: Discovering Christ in the Old Testament* (Phillipsburg, NJ: P&R, 2013), 12.

evidence, *non sequitur* reasoning, and faulty exegesis."[28] Thus, we are faced with two questions which require our immediate attention: What is the nature of the God's covenant with mankind? And what are the end-times? In dealing with our first question, we will also explore the correlation between the concepts of covenant and kingdom. And in our second question, we will examine the OT terms 'Day of the Lord' and the 'latter days,' seeking a distinction with the NT's term 'last days.'

We begin first by asserting that God has dealt with mankind by means of a covenant to save a people for Himself. By this 'voluntary condescension on God's part,' which He planned before time begin, and worked out in successive stages, God has redeemed a special people to be His very own (Confession of Faith 7.1).[29] This unconditional covenant of grace, which forms both the structure and thematic unity of the whole Bible, has been fulfilled through the life, work, death, and resurrection of God's Son Jesus Christ, the God-Man (Lk 22:20). Thus, believers, having received eternal redemption through the blood the everlasting covenant (Gen 15:18; 17:7; Lk 22:20; Heb 13:20), come to Christ and are conveyed by God "into the kingdom of the Son of His love" (Col 1:13; 1 Pet 2:4).

Over against this view, Dispensationalists state emphatically that "the church is a mystery, unrevealed

---

[28] Robert Gundry, *The Church and the Tribulation: A Biblical Examination of Posttribulationism* (Grand Rapids, MI: Zondervan, 1973), 10.
[29] O. Palmer Robertson, *The Christ of the Covenants* (Phillipsburg: P&R, 1980), 47.

in the OT." [30]   However, the church consists of those "called out" (ἐκκλησία) of the world into a covenant fellowship with God. The church is therefore not an aside or parenthesis in God's redemptive plan, it is God's saving program for mankind as well as the culminative number of the elect of all history. Christ's own are therefore kingdom-people and members of the covenant of grace. Thus, the covenant of grace is none other than Christ's kingdom administration whereby, making remedy for Adam's sin, God gathers elect sinners to Himself and enables them to experience the peace, joy, and rest of serving Him in His kingdom forever (Lev 26:11; Jn 1:12).[31] Thus, Hank Hanegraaff rightly observes, "Christianity has always believed in one people of God based on relationship rather than race."[32]

Over against this assertion, Dispensationalism purports a 'race-based' salvation for Jewish people. However, Christ declares: "Do not suppose that you can say to yourselves, 'We have Abraham for our father'; for I say to you, that God is able from these stones to raise up children to Abraham" (Matt 3:9). Grace doesn't run in the blood; God's children are "born not of blood, nor of the will of the flesh, nor of the will of man, but of God" (Jn 1:12-13; 3:3). The relevance of this comes sharply into focus when we consider that it is against both the covenant and the

---

[30] Charles C. Ryrie, *Dispensationalism Today* (Chicago: Moody Press, 1965), 135.
[31] Meredith G. Kline, *Kingdom Prologue: Genesis Foundations for a Covenantal Worldview* (Eugene, OR: Wipf & Stock, 2006), 233.
[32] Hank Hanegraaff, *The Apocalypse Code* (Nashville: Thomas Nelson, 2007), xx.

kingdom of God in which Satan's rage is directed (Dan 7:25; Rev 12:17).

In order to determine when tribulation is to occur, we now move to consider our second question: What are the end-times? The prophets in the OT speak of the "latter days" as a time in which God will restore His people. For example, Malachi declares, "Before the coming of the great and dreadful day of the Lord," the Lord will send Elijah the prophet who will turn the hearts of the fathers and their children to one another (Mal 4:5-6). Jesus identifies John the Baptist as the one coming in the spirit and power of Elijah to accomplish this task of preparing the people for the Lord's coming (Mt 11:14).

Moreover, these "latter days" were to be a time when: (1) God's law would be revealed to the world (Is 2:1-4), (2) the Refiner would purify the "sons of Levi and refine them like gold and silver," enabling them to bring "offerings in righteousness to the Lord" (Mal 3:2-3), and (3) the Messiah would judge between many people (Mic 4:1-5; Mt 10:34). Malachi declares this time of restoration will commence when "the Lord, whom you seek, will suddenly come to His temple" (Mal 3:1). And the prophet asks: But who can endure the day of His coming (Mal 3:2)?

Perhaps the question we should ask is: How are the last days distinguished from the "Day of the Lord?" The OT prophets, by what scholars refer to as "prophetic foreshortening," viewed salvation and judgment as happening together. For example, in Malachi chapter four the prophet declares that the "Day that is coming" burns "like an oven" to consume the proud as "stubble" (Mal 4:1-2). Concomitantly, for those who fear God's name, this day will be unto salvation: "You will trample the wicked" (Mal 4:3). This "Day" that is coming, Malachi says, is a day of both judgment and salvation. Thus, whereas the last days refer to the time of God's gracious restoration of His covenant people, the "Day of the Lord," refers to Christ's second advent.

It is these last days (ἐσχάτου τῶν ἡμερῶν), as the writer to the Book of Hebrews tells us, that God has given mankind His fullest revelation of Himself in the Person of Jesus Christ (Heb 1:2). The 'last days' are therefore the time which God willed and fixed for the redemption of his people, all the elect (Mt 1:21). Thus, we are living in the last days or 'inaugurated end times,' the 'year of Jubilee' in which this present age and the age to come overlap.

This comes into focus for us in the Gospel of Luke when Jesus Himself juxtaposes the "Day of the Lord" with the "last days." As Luke 4:19 records, He quotes from the scroll of Isaiah 61 in the synagogue of Nazareth. Jesus declares that He had been sent "to proclaim the acceptable year of the Lord" and He stops. However, Isaiah 61:2 says: "to proclaim the acceptable year of the Lord, *and the day of vengeance of our God.*" Why didn't Jesus finish the sentence? Jesus didn't finish the sentence because there is a mystery about his coming, namely, that it is a two-act drama.

The first coming of Jesus Christ ushered in the acceptable year of the Lord, a year (a period of time) for salvation through judgment (Jn 3:36). The time we currently live in is a day of God's gracious patience. But this was most unexpected. As Greg Beale observes, "Perhaps one of the most striking features of Jesus's Kingdom is that it appears not to be the kind of kingdom prophesied in the OT and expected by

Judaism."[33] What Israel greatly longed for, and were eagerly in expectation for, was an earthly conqueror, a mighty king that they hoped would vanquish Rome and restore Israel and usher in a physical millennial kingdom. But what they desperately needed was a Savior to deliver them not from earthly physical hardship but from supernatural demonic bondage (Mt 12:29). The logic of pretribulationism is strangely similar to the eschatological expectations of Second Temple Judaism.

The point is, God delays His final judgment until the full number of His people are brought in.[34] Thus, necessitating the church to endure all tribulation. But when the year of Jubilee is over, and the time appointed by the Father has come, then the day of vengeance (Day of the Lord) will arrive and the prophecy of Isaiah 61:2 will be completed. As the apostle Paul declares, "the Lord Jesus will be revealed from heaven with his mighty angels in flaming fire, inflicting vengeance upon those who do not know God and upon those who do not obey the gospel of our Lord Jesus Christ" (2 Thess 1:7-8). This current age will end with the return of Christ, bringing the general resurrection and the final judgment in the 'Day of the Lord' (see diagram below).

---

[33] Gregory K. Beale, *The Book of Revelation* (Grand Rapids, MI: Eerdmans, 1999), 341.
[34] This argument will be developed in chapter five.

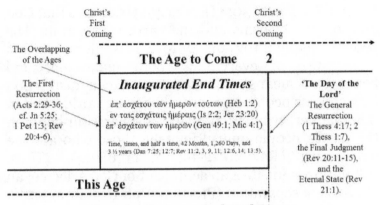

Figure 1. Inaugurated End Times.

Covenant-Tribulation-Exodus

Having examined the concept of covenant and the inaugurated end times, we consider again our first point: Tribulation sovereignly fulfills God's purpose by gathering the elect (by effecting separation). We begin by affirming that it's the Holy Spirit alone, working in and through the Word of God, that the elect are saved. Thus, the elect are gathered by God's Spirit, working when and how He chooses, applying the death and life of Christ to His own (Jn 3:3-8; Act 13:48). Salvation is thus by the eternal decree of God which is applied to us in the gospel by the Holy Spirit. Taken together, in addition to what has been said about suffering, when we say tribulation gathers the elect, it is only in the sense of how it's a playing out of the process of affecting separation and making a distinction (Mt 10:34; cf. Ex 8:23).

Asaph brings out this nuance in Psalm 50. God declares to be coming in devouring fire to save His own who call upon Him in the day of their trouble θλῖψις.

In the LXX, Psalm 50:4 (Psalm 49:4) declares that God calls on the heavens and the earth to 'separate' His people διακρίναι τον λαόν αυτού. This infers that God makes use of everything (both malevolent and benevolent means) in order to make a distinction between His people and the unbelieving world. And in this manner, tribulation affects a separation between the Lord's people and ultimately, those who are the devil's own (Rev 20:12-15; cf. Is 66:24). Thus, tribulation is in effect an acting out of God's decree, an affecting of separation (Pro 16:4; Eph 1:15; Rom 9:22). And God does this by means of a covenant (Gen 15:17-18).

In the Ancient Near-East there were two types of treaties or covenants: A suzerainty treaty and a royal grant treaty.[35] This first type was imposed upon a lesser king and his people by a greater king; often as a result of having been delivered. It was to this great king that a suzerain would swear allegiance by way of particular stipulations. If the suzerain failed to keep all of the stipulations, he and his people would be cut off. And in form and content, the covenant that was sworn at Mt. Sinai was a suzerainty treaty. This first type of covenant was conditional, such as the covenant God made with Adam in Eden, the covenant of works.[36] The reality of the covenant of works is everyone born in Adam are dead, defiled, and damned; and will remain so unless Christ's redemption is applied to them (Mt 11:27). This is because God made a covenant of works

---

[35] Michael Horton, *Introducing Covenant Theology* (Grand Rapids, MI: Baker, 2006), 41.

[36] In Genesis 1-3, Yahweh the great King gave covenant stipulations to Adam which sanctioned death for disobedience and life for obedience.

with Adam and his posterity whereby Adam, and all of us, were promised life for obedience and death for disobedience (Gen 1:28; 2:15-17; Confession of Faith 7.2).

And God's sanctions are carried out against Adam in his exile and later in Israel's exile from the land. Dispensationalism is antithetically opposed to this line of thought. For example, Mal Couch goes as far to say that "the church can only be the new Israel and the inheritor of Israel's promises given in the Abrahamic covenant if either (1) the Abrahamic covenant is shown to be conditional, or (2) the promises of the covenant are spiritualized." [37] We will present our view of the relationship between Israel and the church in chapter three. However, in response to Couch's second comment, we reply the covenant that God makes with Abram in Genesis 15 is quite different from the suzerainty type. God makes the promise that through his Seed all the nations of the earth would be blessed (Gen 3:15; 17:5-7; 22:18; Gal 3:17, 29). And Abraham believed God and it was accounted to him as righteousness (Gen 15:6); God's electing love having created in him the obedience of faith.

In this covenant, God comes to Abraham and He does all the talking. At Sinai, Israel swore an oath before the Lord, but in Genesis 15, God is the One who makes the promise. Genesis 15:13-16 declares:

> Then the Lord said to Abram, "Know for certain that your offspring will be *sojourners* in a land that is not theirs and will be servants there, and they will be

---

[37] Mal Couch, *Dictionary of Premillennial Theology: A Practical Guide to the People, Viewpoints, and History of Prophetic Studies*, (Grand Rapids, MI: Kregel, 1996), 29.

afflicted for four hundred years. But I will bring *judgment on the nation that they serve,* and *afterward they shall come out with great possessions.* As for you, you shall go to your fathers in *peace;* you shall be buried in a good old age. And they shall come back here in the fourth generation, *for the iniquity of the Amorites is not yet complete"* [emphasis added].

What is remarkable is that God is acting on the part of the lesser king in this royal grant treaty.[38] Then in a vision, Abram witnesses God symbolically pass through the parts, 'cutting' the covenant and ratifying His promises (Gen 15:17-18). In a symbolic way, God says in effect "let My own covenant curse fall on Me so that it not fail." And Abraham hoped in the things unseen, that he should become the father of many nations (Rom 4:18).

Moreover, Abram saw that he was not merely the inheritor of the land of promise, but of the world (Rom 4:13). The author of the Book of Hebrews tells us that Abraham acknowledged that he was a "stranger and exile on the earth" waiting for the heavenly fulfillment of the promise; for "the city which has foundations, whose builder and maker is God" (Heb 11:10). And if this weren't 'spiritualized' enough, Hebrews elaborates further that what Abraham (and all the saints) hoped for is a heavenly country, the city of God (Heb 11:16; 12:22-24).

Making the oath to Abram, God in effect swears by His own life that He will perform it: "If I do not keep the oath, may I be divided as these animals."[39] Hence,

---

[38] Michael Horton, *Introducing Covenant Theology,* 33, 42.
[39] Clowney, *The Unfolding Mystery,* 51.

God's covenant with Abram and his Seed was "a pledge to the death."[40] Michael Horton observes:

> It is not that Abraham has no obligations in the covenant relation. Already he has been required to leave his fatherland (Gen 12:1ff). Later he shall be required to administer the seal of circumcision to all his male descendants (Gen 17:1, 4). But as the covenant is instituted formally in Genesis 15, the Lord dramatizes the gracious character of the covenantal relation by having himself alone to pass between the pieces. The covenant shall be fulfilled because God assumes to himself full responsibility in seeing to its realization.[41]

And in the fullness of time, the Son of God bears His own curse on behalf of Abram and his seed (Dt 29:14-15; Gal 4:17, 29).

One of the many things Genesis 15 teaches us is God makes a distinction between His own people and the unbelieving world. Looking again at Gen 15:13-16, we find five key elements which are recapitulated in the exodus from Egypt. These are:

(1) God's covenant people will be sojourners who are afflicted (verse 13).
(2) God will judge the nation that afflicts them (verse 14).
(3) God's covenant people come out with great possessions (verse 14).
(4) The death of the elect will be as Abraham's (verse 15).
(5) The destruction of the wicked coincides with the deliverance of the righteous (verse 16).

---

[40] Horton, *Introducing Covenant Theology*, 146.
[41] Ibid., 65.

When we come to the Book of Exodus, we find God reaffirming His covenant promises to His people through the prophet Moses. The people are being afflicted, living as sojourners in a land not their own (Ex 1:8-9; 3:9). This tribulation is brought on due to their covenant loyalty. But, seeing their affliction and distress at the hands of the Egyptians, God unsheathes His sword and through ten plagues, executes His judgments in order to bring His people to Himself.

The Exodus from Egypt may be seen to be redemption through divine warfare.[42]   The whole ordeal centered on whether Israel would be permitted to worship God or not. For behind Pharaoh's stubborn refusal was the devil's desire to prevent the worship God (Ex 5:1-2). But this was expressly the Lord's purpose in bringing out a people (collectively referred to as "My son") is so they may serve λατρεύσῃ Him (Ex 4:23; Mt 2:15; cf. Hos 11:1).[43]

Then to Moses, God said, "I will take you to be My people, and I will be your God (Ex 6:7; Lev 26:11-13). God's gracious covenant is based in and on His promises to keep mercy to thousands; to those who love Him and keep Him commandments. That is, as the LXX puts it, God keeps His covenant love חֶסֶד *unto the thousandth generation* (Ex 20:6; 33:19; 34:7).[44]

---

[42] Tremper Longman III and Daniel G. Reid, *God is a Warrior* (Grand Rapids, MI: Zondervan, 1995), 91-92.

[43] In his gospel, Matthew uses Christ's coming out of Egypt to corporately identify all of God's covenant people with Jesus Christ who is Himself true Israel, God's Servant.

[44] Hesed occurring 247 times in the Old Testament, is used by the Scripture to convey the love and loyalty God bears to His gracious covenant. Additionally, *hesed* describes love for God and man (Dt 6:5; Lev 19:18).

In dramatic fashion, following the miraculous Red Sea crossing and subsequent destruction of the Egyptian Army, Moses looks into the whole of future history and prophesies of God's covenant love: "You have led in your steadfast love (*hesed*) the people whom you have redeemed; you have guided them by your strength to your holy abode (Ex 15:13). With a mighty hand, God brings His people out of bondage and declares, I will show My covenant love (*hesed*) "to those who love Me and keep My commandments," unto the thousandth generation (LXX Ex 20:6).

Reflecting on the exodus, Deuteronomy 4:34 declares that God took "a nation for himself from the midst of another nation, by trials, by signs, by wonders, and by war, by a mighty hand and an outstretched arm, and by great deeds of terror." Fighting to bring His people out of the iron furnace, God is said to have let loose on the Egyptians "his burning anger, wrath, indignation, and distress" (Ps 78:49). According to Psalm 78, the judgement on Egypt was executed in some measure by "a company of destroying angels" (Ps 78:49). If we ask: Were these 'destroying angels' elect or fallen? We are reminded that God "does according to His will in the army of heaven" (Dan 4:35). Thus, all creatures, actions and things whether benevolent or malevolent are wisely employed by God unto His glory (Confession of Faith 5.7).

The point is, God employed various forms of tribulation through diverse agents in ten tremendously awesome plagues in order to affect separation, "make a distinction" between His people and Pharaoh's (Ex 8:23). And exacting judgment on Egypt and the gods of Egypt (Ex 12:12), God led out (ἐξάγω) His own (Ex 12:31; Dt 4:20). In passing, the exodus account also

29

teaches us that a form of tribulation God's people face is due to their covenant loyalty in the face of external persecution by the state (Ex 1:15-22; 2:1-3; 5:17-21; Rev 13:7).

We now move to consider our second point: Tribulation sovereignly fulfills God's purpose by purifying and strengthening the elect. To begin with, it may be said that Israel's affliction in Egypt was proof of their election (Ex 8:23; cf. 2 Thess 1:5). And ultimately, tribulation strengthened God's people during the exodus as their faith in God deepened with each act of His preservation during the judgment plagues (Dt 4:34); God uses tribulation to create staying power.

A good question at this point is: What sustained God's covenant people in tribulation? Faith and God's covenantal seal.[45] Moreover, the witness of the saints, through Moses and Aaron, as well as the covenant faithfulness of Israel expressed in belief, continued up to and during the last plague (Ex 10:3). During the plagues, a mixed multitude of Gentiles joined themselves to Israel and departed in the exodus (Ex 12:38-39). This episode itself demonstrates God's plan to take for Himself a people from all nations (Rev 7:9).

In consideration of our third point, tribulation sovereignly fulfills God's purpose by serving as the means for hardening and judging the reprobate. The point is, tribulation not only affects separation between God's people and the world, it also serves as the means for God's retributive justice toward the reprobate. The basis for the judgment of the wicked is first and

---

[45] John Calvin, *Commentary on the Second Epistle to the Thessalonians*, vol. 21 (Grand Rapids, MI: Baker, 2009), 312.

foremost their disobedience to God, lack of faith in Christ, and secondarily their treatment of God's covenant people (Gen 15:16; Mt 26:31-46). Thus, God's retributive justice against His enemies is determined according to *lex talionis* (law of retaliation), whereby the wicked reap the reward for their labor. Expounding this concept, Joshua Owen explains:

> The justice that is celebrated in the consummation of the kingdom of Christ is measured according to the *lex talionis* as both compensation and punishment. In terms of compensation, the servants of God are rewarded, at least in part, with vindication for the unjust condemnation they endured by their persecutors. In terms of judgment, the persecutors of the church receive precisely what they inflicted, wrath and destruction.[46]

An further facet merits notice. The salvation of the full number of God's people coincides with the destruction of the wicked (Ps 37:28; Pro 14:11). This seems to be the deeper meaning behind Gen 15:16 in which God declares the seed of Abraham will be brought out as the iniquity of the wicked reaches its fullness (Gen 15:16; cf. Lev 18:24-25; Mt 23:32; 1 Thess 2:16). From a historical standpoint, this occurred several times: First, when God destroyed the firstborn of Egypt and saved Israel, His firstborn; then, when He drowned the Egyptians in the Red sea, while the Israelites passed safely through it; and further when

---

[46] Joshua Owen, "Martyrdom as an Impetus for Divine Retribution in the Book of Revelation" available from http://digital.library.sbts.edu/handle/10392/479; Internet; accessed 14 July 2016.

the 'Amorites' are given over to destruction in the conquest of Canaan (Gen 15:16); not to mention Noah (Gen 7:23) and Lot (Gen 19:29).

Perhaps this is what the Bible refers to when it declares the destruction of the God's enemies makes a way for the salvation of His elect (Pro 11:8; Is 43:3)? Ultimately, mediate judgments are divine warnings which serve as types of the final judgment which befall the wicked at the end of this age (Mt 24:37; Rev 20:11-15). Thus, God brings talionic mediate judgment upon unbelievers while there yet remains a future final judgment.[47]

Additionally, when God announces He will take vengeance on the Egyptians in Gen 15:14, He declares He will in the same manner render to all the enemies of His people, who are in fact His enemies (Zech 2:8). This is expressly stated in the Song of Moses, where the enemies of God are extended to include the pagan nations of the world (Dt 32:34-36; cf. Is 30:27-33; Jer 9:25). Thus, an attack on God's people is an attack on God Himself (Acts 9:4-5; Mt 25:40), this is because through the afflictions of His people, God Himself is said to suffer (Is 63:9; Mt 25:45; Col 1:24).

Correlating the exodus with tribulation, we may surmise the following:

(1) Tribulation was the means God used to effect separation between Israel and Egypt (Ex 8:23; 11:7).
(2) The faith of God's people became grounded and increased as they were preserved and delivered through tribulation which in the ten plagues took on the form of God's retributive justice (Ex 6:6).

---

[47] Ladd, *The Presence of the Future*, 120.

(3) God's covenant people were preserved through wrath and came out only after the final plague had been executed (Ex 12:23). *In like manner, the church will remain in the world until Christ's second coming.*

In light of the above, covenant-tribulation-exodus coalesce in God's infinite wisdom to create a holy nation who serve (λατρεύση), worship Him as a kingdom of mediating priests, who not only endure persecution, but persevere and are blessed in spite of it; "The more they were oppressed, the more they multiplied and the more they spread abroad" (Ex 1:11-12). Tribulation was the means to gather the covenant people as God through judgment made a distinction, afflicting those who afflicted His people, given them over to destruction (Ex 7:3-5; 2 Thess 1:6).

We are further reminded of the fact that when the Bible elaborates on the meaning of the exodus, it is discussed not only as a historical event, but also a prophetic event, as Jindřich Mánek observes "God's future actions were often interpreted in the spirit of the Exodus from Egypt."[48] We move now to consider God's agent of this exodus.

The Suffering Servant

In the Book of Isaiah, the prophet introduces us to God's elect One, the suffering Servant, whose task is to *fulfill the covenant, render judgment,* and *bring in everlasting righteousness* (Dan 9:24-27).[49]   The

---

[48] Jindřich Mánek, "The New Exodus in the Books of Luke" *Novum Testamentum* 2 (1957): 8-23.

[49] It is my understanding that there are five songs: (1) Is 42:1-4; (2) 49:1-6; (3) 50:4-9; (4) 52:13-53:12; (5) 61:1-3.

suffering Servant is the One through whom God's righteous purpose is finally realized. In the Book of Isaiah, the five songs illustrate the three-fold task of the Servant: (1) fulfill the covenant by confirming and strengthening it (Is 42:6; 52:13-53:12; Dan 9:27); (2) render a true judgment that Yahweh alone is to be worshipped, the gods of other nations are in reality demons (Is 49:1-6; cf. Dt 32:17; 1 Cor 10:10);[50] and (3) bring in everlasting righteousness by revealing God's Law and establishing God's just order – the Kingdom of God (Is 61:1-3).

First, the Servant confirmed and strengthened the covenant of grace. As O. Palmer Robertson put it, a covenant is "a bond in bold sovereignly administered."[51] This Servant, Isaiah declares, will Himself be a covenant, that is, He will be the means through whom people come into covenant relationship with the Triune God; "I will give you as a covenant for the people, a light for the nations, to open the eyes that are blind, to bring out the prisoners from the dungeon, from the prison those who sit in darkness" (Is 42:6-7). This is precisely what Daniel 9:24-27 (the so-called 70 Weeks) is all about; "And He shall *strengthen* the covenant with the many for one week" (Dan 9:27; cf. Mt 26:28; Heb 8:13). Space will not permit a full argument, suffice it to say that what Christ *has already accomplished* in His life, death, and resurrection, *viz.*, in the seventieth week of Daniel 9:24-27, *will continue to have its effects* until His second advent.[52]

---

[50] Longman, *God is a Warrior*, 142.

[51] O. Palmer Robertson, *The Christ of the Covenants* (Phillipsburg, NJ: P&R, 1980), 4.

[52] Edward J. Young, *The Prophecy of Daniel: A Commentary* (Grand Rapids, MI: Eerdmans, 1949), 208-209.

Second, the Servant settles a true judgment and renders a verdict: "He will bring forth justice to the nations" (Is 42:1). The elect Servant's mission is in effect, an acting out of God's decree, bringing a separating trial; a contest which will divide the nations, and gather God's elect (cf. Mt 10:34). The task of the suffering Servant is to inaugurate God's end time judgment, resulting in tribulation. This resultant tribulation takes on two forms: talionic justice and demonic rage.

In the first sense, as an expression of God's righteous anger, tribulation takes on the form of talionic justice or vengeance. In the OT, this is expressed in various ways. In Leviticus 26, it comes against apostates as 'vengeance of the covenant' (Lev 26:35; cf. Dt 32). And in the NT, it is paid back to the reprobate for their unjust treatment of Christ and His own (Mt 25:41-46; cf. Rev 6:3-11). In the second sense, the coming of the suffering Servant brings a contest of spiritual warfare. The Servant liberates captives (Is 43:7-10; 49:24-25) while the powers of darkness seek to resist Him and counterattack with deception and persecution, "He who does not *gather* with Me scatters abroad" (Mt 12:29-30; 13:21; Rev 12:16). And thirdly, God the Son proclaims the Kingdom of God, revealing God's Law, first in the mouths of His prophets of old then in the fullness of time through His own mouth and His apostles by proclaiming the kingdom of God (Mt 28:18-20).

Isaianic Second Exodus

Whereas at the exodus, God judged the gods of Egypt, plundered their spoils, and restored His people to Himself (Gen 15:14-16; Ex 12:12; 15:13), through His suffering Servant, God announces a new exodus will occur, which will not only accomplish the same, but in a new and elevated sense, will further lead to the purification of His covenant people, in the midst of whom He will reign in a restored Jerusalem-Zion (Ps 2:6-9; Gal 4:26; Heb 12:22-24). This is the very essence of what Christ accomplished in His First Advent. He bound the strong man, and began liberating the captives by calling them out of darkness into His marvelous light (Mt 12:28-29; Jn 14:15).

As prophesied by Isaiah (some two hundred years before he was born), Cyrus was chosen by God to deliver the Lord's covenant people by overthrowing Babylon thus liberating them in order to build both Jerusalem and the temple (Is 44:28; 45:1). Cyrus is astonishingly referred מְשִׁיחוֹ *mashiach* messiah (Is 45:1) and shepherd (Is 44:28). As the chosen shepherd (Is 44:28), the Lord declares, "He shall build My city and let My exiles go free" (Is 45:13; cf. Dan 9:25). Thus, the rise of Cyrus (Is 44:28; 45:13), the coming judgment on Babylon (Is 47:1-3), and the release of the exiles (Is 29:18) correlates to the exodus: judgment to release captives.

It may be summarized by saying: Whereas, in the first exodus, God delivered His covenant nation out of a nation, He now delivers His covenant nation out of the nations of the earth (1 Pet 2:9). Likewise, as the first exodus was a deliverance from physical bondage, the new exodus is one from spiritual bondage. Christ now delivers His covenant people, who consist of everyone He died for from every tribe, tongue, people, and nation (Is 56:3-8; Mt 26:28; Rev 7:9). The diagram below demonstrates this line of thought:

36

First Exodus

Deliverer	Means of Deliverance	Result	Terminus
Moses	Judgment Plagues	Release of Physical Captives	Sinai

Isaianic New Exodus Antitype

Deliverer	Means of Deliverance	Result	Terminus
Cyrus	Judgment on Babylon	Release of Physical Captives	Jerusalem

New Exodus

Deliverer	Means of Deliverance	Result	Terminus
Jesus Christ	Binding of Satan & Judgment on the Nations	Release of Spiritual Captives	New Heavens & New Earth

Figure 2. Exodus Types and the New Exodus.

At this point, some may object that we are spiritualizing away such promises as the land. So what about the land promises? The short answer is: What the church has believed and taught for twenty centuries is the New Testament equivalent of the "land" is the whole world, in Christ, and ultimately the new earth. God's people are given the whole earth as an inheritance (Rom 4:13).

Over against this view, in addition to envisioning two redemptive programs: one for Israel and one for the church, Dispensationalism understands most (if not all) of the land promises to be unfulfilled. For example, John Walvoord states emphatically:

> The Scriptures demand a future fulfillment of the prophecies relating to Israel, that Israel will be restored as a nation and regathered to the land of Palestine, that the promises to Abraham regarding the possession of the land by his seed will be fulfilled by Israel, that the promise to David regarding his throne will be fulfilled by the return of Christ to reign

37

on the earth, that the prophetic foreview of a glorious and righteous kingdom on earth will be fulfilled through the return and reign of Christ, and that there will be a literal millennium on earth before the eternal state.[53]

However, in order to understand the land promise, we must understand the manner in which the NT uses the OT. For without an understanding of the new covenant and what Christ has accomplished, we will be lost.

First, it may be said that the land promises to Israel have already been fulfilled. In the Book of Joshua, following the conquest of Canaan, the Spirit declares:

> Thus the Lord gave to Israel all the land that he swore to give to their fathers. And they took possession of it, and they settled there. And the Lord gave them rest on every side just as he had sworn to their fathers. Not one of all their enemies had withstood them, for the Lord had given all their enemies into their hands. Not one word of all the good promises that the Lord had made to the house of Israel had failed; all came to pass (Joshua 21:43-45).

Thus all the land promises God made to Israel through Moses have already been fulfilled (cf. 1 Kgs 8:56).

Secondly, it should be remembered that the land belongs to the Lord of the covenant, as God declares in Leviticus 25:23: "The land is mine, and you are

---

53 John F. Walvoord, "Eschatological Problems V: Is the Church the Israel of God" available from http://walvoord.com/article/22; Internet; accessed 14 July 2016.

strangers and tenants with Me" (cf. Mt 21:33-44).[54] In the NT we our taught that the Lord Jesus possess the whole of heaven and the earth: "For the earth is the Lord's and everything in it" (1 Cor 10:26).

Under the new covenant, the Word of God declares Abraham to be heir not of the land, but of the world (Rom 4:13). In the new covenant, the land concept is therefore expanded to include the cosmos and so our inheritance is the new heavens and the new earth (Mt 5:5). "By this comprehensive language," observes O. Palmer Robertson, "the imagery of land as a picture of restored paradise has finally come of age. No longer merely a portion of this earth, but now the whole of the cosmos partakes of the consummation of God's redemptive work in our fallen world."[55]

Space prevents a full argument. However, suffice it to say that in the OT, the land of Israel was holy solely for the fact that God was said to inhabit it. The Lord charged Israel not to defile the land, because He said "I dwell in the midst of my people" (Num 35:34). Because of the Canaanites' abominations the land vomited them out (Lev 18:25; cf. Gen 15:16).

Israel was admonished to be careful to keep the Lord's commandments or the land would likewise vomit them out (Lev 18:28; 20:22).[56] The Bible teaches that when Adam and Eve rebelled, they lost their right to the Garden and God cast them out. God used the very same principle with Israel. He gave them the land, but warning them over and over again that if they rebelled, they would be cast out. God's people ignored

---

54 Robertson, *The Israel of God, Yesterday, Today and Tomorrow*, 8.
55 Ibid, 26.
56 Ibid, 12.

the prophets and for their covenant disloyalty they went into exile for 70 years (Jer 34:17-20; 39: 9).

The 70 years was the exact number of Sabbatical years in a four hundred and ninety year period. It also corresponds to 10 jubilees. It seems most likely that this period of 490 years is reckoned from the destruction of the tabernacle in Shiloh during the time of the Judges to the destruction of the temple in 586 BC (Ps 78:56-60). The seventy years captivity began when Jerusalem was raised and the temple was destroyed in 586 BC. These 70 years ended in 516 BC when the second temple was finished.

Just as God forsook Shiloh, the place where He had placed His name at first, the place where the priests had no fear for the Almighty and profaned His altar, losing the Ark of the Covenant in battle, God then forsook Jerusalem, as they had forsaken Him. God prepares a stock lament for them in advance: "A voice of wailing is heard from Zion: How we are plundered! Because we have forsaken the land, because we have been cast out of our dwellings" (Jer 9:19).

The ironic thing about the exile is, it is those who go into captivity who are regarded by God as "good," while the "bad" are those who remain (Jer 24:1-10). And it will be through sufferings that God's people will learn that He watches over them for good. God protects His people. Even in Babylon God will watch over them and will not allow them to suffer alone. If you want proof, consider how God protected Daniel's friends Haniniah, Meshiael, and Azariah or Shadrach, Meshach, and Abednego (Dan 3).

The OT prophets declared that Israel would come out of exile, and indeed they did. However, it was hardly on the grand scale prophesied. In light of this, it must be understood that the OT promises about exiles coming back to the Promised Land, are interpreted in the NT, without exception, as Gentiles coming into the Christian church. In the exile, God promised to restore Israel to Himself as a holy nation, a royal priesthood, a kingdom of priests, and the NT applies this promise to the church (Is 61:6; Zech 3:6; 1 Pet 2:9). Further, we are reminded of the purpose of the exile, which was to purge away rebels from among the Lord's covenant people so as to purify a holy remnant for Himself (Dt 8:2; Is 1:4-6; cf. Ezek 20:37-38; Rom 11:5). And this cleansing enables returning.

There is an exodus adumbration in the OT which foreshadows the recovery of captives along with the plundering of the enemy. This incident occurred when Abraham recovered Lot and his fellow captives in a night raid on the marauding army of Chedolaomar (Gen 14:12-24). This served not only as a type for the exodus, but further as a type of second exodus in that Abram gave a tenth of the spoils to the priest-king Melchizedek (Gen 14:20). He then gave to God via Melchizadek a 'tenth' of the spoils, leaving the remainder to fall back into the hands of the king of Sodom (Gen 14:20-24).

What's pertinent to our discussion is the fact that Abraham's military exploit serves as a prophetic adumbration of Christ's deliverance, *viz.*, Abraham rescued his kinsmen who were lost and held captive by the enemy and delivering them, returned bearing them as lost vessels (Is 52:11; 53:12; Mt 12:29). Likewise, by the work of the suffering Servant, the blind and the deaf both see and hear and return to Zion with singing, bearing along with them the vessels of the Lord – those we have won for Christ (Is 52:11).

In Christ, we therefore experience a new exodus, a promised rest that is of the soul as we are gathered into one holy temple by the Spirit (1 Pet 2:4).

To add a further facet, the Book of Hebrews declares that long after the original entrance into the Land of Promise was achieved, King David spoke of another 'rest' that could be entered and enjoyed or lost. Echoing Psalm 95, the author of the Book of Hebrews declares: "There remains therefore a rest for the people of God." In Christ we have a 'positional rest' in which we await a future consummated rest, as Greg Beale observes:

> Christians begin now to enjoy existentially a Sabbath rest by virtue of our real inaugurated resurrection life which has been communicated to us through the life-giving Spirit. But our rest is still incomplete because our resurrection existence has begun only spiritually and has not been consummated bodily.[57]

To summarize, in the words of O. Palmer Robertson, "The possession of the land under the old covenant was not an end in itself, but fit instead among the shadows, types, and prophecies that were characteristic of the old covenant in its presentation of redemptive truth."[58] We are therefore reminded that in Christ, all the promises of God, including everything the land pointed to, are yes and amen (2 Cor 1:22). Moreover, as exiles, we are given a new heart to know God (Jer 24:7; 31:33; 32:38-40). We keep the Passover and continue to come out of the nations to Christ, and thus constitute

---

[57] Beale, *The Temple and the Church's Mission*, 293-312.
[58] O. Palmer Robertson, *The Israel of God, Yesterday, Today and Tomorrow* (Phillipsburg, NJ: P&R, 2000), 13.

the true temple-Zion.[59] Christ is the true temple and believers are living stones of the true temple.

Getting back to our theme, tribulation also comes from within the covenant community. In OT Israel, social injustice, rampant immorality, and idolatrous worship flourished. Into this religious and social chaos, the prophets were sent as God's covenant prosecutors. The repeated refrain of the OT is the coming judgment for Israel's covenant infidelity. The prophets brought a charge, a *rib* (contention) against Israel for her covenant unfaithfulness. The prophets announced covenant judgment in two basic forms: terrestrial, drought, pestilence, famine, disease, population loss; and war, defeat, siege, occupation, death, destruction, and exile, *the four-fold covenant curse* (Deut. 4:25-28; 28:15-68; 29:16-29; 32:15-43; Lev 26:14-39).

In Israel's history, despite her political wrangling, judgment comes by way of Assyria and Babylon. However, there is a remnant chosen by grace who will experience God's forgiveness and mercy. And through God's punitive restorative love, He brings his people into a second exile which will be a time and place for a new bonding of Yahweh with His people.[60] It is out of this place of exile that God calls His Son Jesus Christ and all those who are included in Him (Hos 11:1; Mt 2:15; cf. Ex 4:22; Ps 74:19-20). Thus, the desert is both a place of preservation and testing. It is here that God's people will come to know Him, as God cures His people's waywardness (Hos 2:14; Rev 12:14). The point

---

[59] Alec Motyer, *The Prophecy of Isaiah* (Downers Grove: IVP, 1993), 422.
[60] Willem VanGemeren, *Interpreting the Prophetic Word* (Grand Rapids, MI: Zondervan, 1990), 115.

is, while apostates are destroyed by the sword, the elect survive the sword and going into exile, find grace in the wilderness (Jer 31:1).[61]

Eschatological Birth Pangs of the Messianic Community

One of the ways the Bible pictures God's people in tribulation is that of a barren woman. Zion, God's bride is wearied by her inability to adequately declare God's judgment (Is 26:9-11) or give birth to her promised spiritual children (Is 26:16-18; cf. Gal 4:19, 27; Rev 12:2).[62] And though she is experiencing the pangs (ὠδίνω) of childbirth, as it were without delivering, she is exhorted to trust in the coming deliverance (Is 26:20-21), which will be executed by the sword of the Lord (Is 26:20-27:1; cf. Mt 10:34).

Then, in Isaiah 54, God declares to the woman Zion to break forth into songs of worship, because the work of the suffering Servant has produced for her 'spiritual' children (Is 54:1; cf. Is 53:10-11). The resulting work of the suffering Servant is that many servants are raised up and are gathered to Zion where they 'populate' the dead cities of the nations with the living (Is 54:3; cf. Mt 28:18-20). When we encounter these birth pangs again in the NT, the term is used to refer to the ingathering of the messianic community despite tribulation (Mt 24:8; Rev 12).

---

[61] God paradoxically declares this truth to Jeremiah: Those who go into exile are regarded as "good" while the rest are given over to the covenant curse and are destroyed (Jer 24:4-10).

[62] Conrad Gempf, "The Imagery of Birth pangs in the NT" *Tyndale Bulletin* 45 (1994): 119-135.

God's Seal in Ezekiel 9

The Bible declares that God's people will be preserved spiritually as they encounter tribulation (Rev 3:10; 7:2). Perhaps the locus classicus for this discussion in the OT is Ezekiel 9. The setting is apostate Israel just prior to the leveling of Jerusalem and the destruction of the first temple. And in parabolic form, immersed in apocalyptic typology, the prophet's vision paints a verbal picture of salvation through judgment. The Lord calls for those "who have charge over the city" to draw near "each with his destroying weapon in his hand" (Ezek 9:1). Upon God's command, six angelic beings appear with deadly weapons in their hands. Among them is one with a writing instrument. This one is commanded to go through the city of Jerusalem and place a 'mark' on the foreheads of those who "sigh and groan over all the abominations that are committed in it" (Ezek 9:4).

After him, those with slaughtering instruments are commanded to kill with death those without the mark, beginning in the temple (1 Pet 4:17). When we come to the Book of Revelation, in similar fashion, John's angelic agent places a seal on the foreheads of God servants before the destroying angelic agents are permitted to harm the earth and sea (Rev 7:1-4; 16:2; Eph 1:13; cf. Rev 9:4). The obvious point is: *God preserves his people through wrath by virtue of His covenantal seal.*

Tribulation and the Book of Job

No discussion of tribulation would be complete without a look at the Book of Job which tackles two crucial issues: the problem of suffering and the sovereignty of God. Perhaps the key question in the book of Job is: "Can a righteous person hold on to their faith in God when things go terribly wrong" (Job 1:11; 2:5, 9)? And while Job does hold on to his faith despite his suffering and humiliation, he does not always respond the way he should (Job 32:1-4).

The Book of Job highlights many weighty lessons, some of which are: (1) there is such a thing as innocent suffering, (2) the way we respond to suffering matters, and (3) our suffering can be a means of grace for others. The first lesson is what Job's friends had to learn: tragedy does not befall Job because of his own sin. Their retribution theology was flawed; "sinners suffer, therefore sufferers are sinners."[63]   Moreover, as Tremper Longman observes, "the Book of Job serves as an example to warn us against judging others on the basis of their situation in life."[64]   In the end, Job repents not of sin that got him into his trouble, but of his attitude; thus demonstrating the way we respond to suffering matters (Job 42:5-6).

Perhaps the biggest lesson in Job is the manner in which the innocent sufferings of believers can be a means of grace for others. As has been said, suffering affords God the opportunity to manifest His grace. At the end of Job's trial, as directed by God and as of sign of his friend's repentance, Job serves as a mediating priest and offers sacrifice and intercessory prayer on their behalf (Job 42:7-8). The gracious result is God's wrath meant for Job's friends, who had not spoken

---

[63] Tremper Longman III, *Job* (Grand Rapids, MI: Baker, 2012), 63. Job, it may be said, argues a good case poorly while his friends argue a poor case well (Calvin).
[64] Ibid., 67.

what was right about God, is turned away because of Job's priestly intercession which the Lord accepted (Job 42:9-10). What's clear to see is the manner in which Job serves as a type of Christ by his innocent suffering; his afflictions making a way for the restoration of others who are under the wrath of God (Job 42:7; Jn 3:36).

As we now turn to consider what the NT has to teach us regarding tribulation, we are reminded that in times of suffering, our circumstances are related to "the purpose of the Lord," as part of God's working out His divine purpose in our lives (Jam 5:11; Rom 8:28-29). This is what kept Job slipping away into utter despair and perhaps suicide; "For I know that my Redeemer lives" (Job 19:25-27). Thus, Job answers the question: Can we continue to serve God faithfully even if it means tribulation for us?

Chapter Three:
Tribulation in the New Testament

"In the world you will have tribulation. But take heart; I have overcome the world" (John 16:33).

By the time of the earthly ministry of Jesus, the OT religion of grace had degenerated into a rigid, external, legalistic, works righteousness.[65] It was a far cry from the understanding of the law lived by the patriarchs, which as we've seen, was a religion of grace, based in and on the promises of God (Gen 15; Ex 20:2-6). But the people, lifting the law out of its gracious roots, were preserving the external practices of worship without its essential heart.

New Covenant

When Jesus confronted the legal precisionists of the day He referred them to Hosea 6:6: "I desire mercy (covenant loyalty-love LXX) and not sacrifice." God truly delights in reciprocal covenant-love (*hesed*) and not sacrifice divorced from grace.[66] By God's design, covenant living is to be motivated by a love for God and man, which works itself out in obedient faith, and is anchored in God's unchangeable covenant promise (Gen 15:6). What pleases God more, said Jesus, is not the external form of worship, which pointed to Himself, but rather its essence which is love for God,

---

[65] Second Temple Judaism (the religion of the Jews between 516 BC and 70 AD), is a name widely used to define this period.
[66] Michael P.V. Barrett, "Hosea: His Marriage and His Message" *Puritan Reformed Journal* 3, no. 2 (2011): 11.

pouring out in love for our neighbor. Jesus says religion without love is nauseating (Is 1:13; Rev 3:16).

Into mankind's plight, Christ, the God-Man, by His perfect obedience, strengthened and confirmed a covenant with many, making a new covenant in His own blood, and put an end to sacrifice after He had offered one sacrifice for sins forever (Is 53:11-12; Dan 9:27; Heb 9:28; 10:12-14). Jesus fulfilled God's original purpose for creation, and in Him, God is recreating humanity, the true Israel (2 Cor 5:17). Whereas, all die in Adam's disobedience, all of God's purchased possession are freely imputed with Christ's righteous obedience, being justified by His grace (Rom 5:12). Thus, the righteousness of God is God's incarnate obedience, an act of God in human nature fulfilling the covenant from man's side (Gen 15:12-21; Rom 4:13; Heb 9:11-15).

Jesus restores true Israel in Himself, fulfills the compact earlier ratified with Abram, and successfully recapitulates Adam's and Israel's role by resisting the devil's temptations, and perfectly fulfilling God's required obedience (Heb 2:10-18; Confession of Faith 8.6).[67] And similar to the prophets of old, Christ, levels the inaugurated end-times *rib* against those of the broken covenant, contending with Israel's covenant unfaithfulness (Mt 21:36-37). Thus, the coming of the Son of Man brings judgment resulting in spiritual warfare and tribulation (Jn 12:31).

---

[67] Over against this, and contrary to the plain teaching of the Word of God, Dispensationalists purport there to be two new covenants (Lewis Sperry Chafer and John F. Walvoord, *Major Bible Themes* (Grand Rapids, MI: Zondervan, 1974), 147.

New Exodus

Christ's coming settles a true judgment, a verdict, a decision rendered which affects a separation (Mt 10:34); a sifting (Hag 2:6-7), and winnowing trial (Is 41:15-16; Mt 3:12). John tells us that the reason the Son of God was manifested was to destroy the works of the devil (1 Jn 3:8). Jesus the suffering Servant, fulfills His heavenly mission by invading the earthly city of man, ruled by his powerful adversary Satan, defeating him through the cross, and began the process of plundering his house by liberating oppressed captives (Lk 4:18-19).[68] Thus, the new exodus is by virtue of a new covenant (Is 55:3; cf. Jer 31:32; Mt 26:28). Whereas, during the exodus, God protected and guided Israel, being both her vanguard and rear guard, by a pillar of fire and cloud (cf. Ex. 13:21-22; 14:19-20), likewise, in the new exodus, the Lord Himself is a consuming fire (Heb 12:29; cf. Zech 2:5).[69]

Ultimately we have the assurance that a perfect atonement secures as the Lord Jesus Himself leads us out of captivity to the endless Sabbath, the eternal rest (Mic 2:10-13; Jn 10:4, 16). In this new exodus, believers presently advance the Kingdom of God through worship, witness and worthy living (Rev 12:11), as they mediate Christ's presence and bear along the treasure that will adorn God's holy temple – His own people (Is 52:11-12; cf. Gen 14:16).

---

[68] Christ fulfills a threefold office of Prophet, Priest and King. Christ perfectly fulfills the will of the Father by revealing God to men (Prophet), by redeeming men from sin (Priest) and by restoring man to God (King).
[69] Longman, *God is a Warrior*, 95.

The Dispensational view runs counter to this by not only asserting that Israel and the church are distinct entities, and that the messianic kingdom awaits Christ's second coming, but there is to be a rebuilt temple in Jerusalem.[70] However, the NT declares the church is the temple (1 Pet 2:4-5); the church are the true Jews (Rom 2:28-29; Phil 3:3). In Christ, believers are the inheritors to everything God ever promised to His people (Gal 3:29). We stand in the same line as Abraham not because we have his blood in our veins but because we have the same faith as he had as well as the same grace of God in our lives (Gal 3:7, 29; Phil 3:3; Col 2:11).

A question that moves our discussion forward is: What is the correlation between judgment and tribulation? It may be said that judgment therefore brings tribulation. For all tribulation is based upon Christ's finished atoning work on Calvary. Judgment is the acting out of God's decree, and tribulation ensues and is a manifestation of the judgment (Rev 5:3). As noted earlier, tribulation is an end time trial which has already been set in motion by Christ's first advent and will culminate with His second advent. To answer our question, we may say: whereas tribulation has been the experience of the church since Abel, the great tribulation is the experience of the church in these last days (ἐσχάτου τῶν ἡμερῶν), which will continue until all Israel is saved and Christ returns (Heb 1:2; cf. Mic 4:1).[71]

In light of this eschatological in-breaking of Christ's judgment and kingdom, it would be prudent to

---

[70] Ice, *The Return*, 28-53.
[71] Hebrews 1:2 declares we are already living in the last days.

remember two important scriptural truths: (1) Christ has already absorbed the wrath of God for His elect (Jn 3:16, 36), and (2) there yet remains a future judgment where everyone who is not included in Christ will suffer eternal punishment (Acts 17:31; Rev 20:11-15). As we have seen, Christ's own are kingdom-people, and as such, they are called to live faithfully within a covenant fellowship with the Triune God and endure tribulation which comes by way of loyalty to the covenant (Lev 26:11; Gal 3:16, 26-29; 4:26, 29). This is topic of our next discussion.

The Suffering Servants

Christ's atoning death and resurrection has accomplished Israel's new exodus redemption. Through the gospel proclamation, Christ brings life and peace for those who receive Him while a damnatory sentence remains on those who reject Him (Jn 3:36). As we approach the NT's teaching on tribulation we are reminded of God's purpose in tribulation to: (1) effect separation and make a distinction unto the purifying and strengthening the elect, (2) serve as the means for hardening and judging the reprobate, as well as (3) affording the saints an opportunity to testify unto the effectual gathering of all the elect.[72]

Looking again to our first point, we are reminded that when we say tribulation gathers the elect, it is only in the sense of how tribulation is a playing out of the process of effecting separation and making a

---

[72] From our earlier discussion in chapter two, I have purposely inverted points one and three.

distinction (Ex 8:23; Mt 10:34).[73]   Christ brings
salvation through judgment, and the mission of the
suffering Servant is now being undertaken by Christ's
followers – the suffering servants (Acts 13:47). What
we've tried to make abundantly clear thus far is
tribulation results on account of the gospel message
that is proclaimed and lived out (Ex 1:11; Rev 12:11; cf.
Rev 14:6). The Bible refers to this as *hesed* covenant
loyalty. And Jesus instructs us, a believer's continued
loyalty to Him will result in persecution (Mt 5:11; 2 Tim
3:12). When we take a stand for Christ we will suffer
demonic attack and incur the world's enmity.

As we've stated, the Bible reveals to us that there is a
cosmic battle between Christ and Satan; persecution
will inevitably result when the gospel is presented. For
as Dietrich Bonhoeffer once observed, "the cross is the
peace of Christ, but it's also a sword God wields on the
earth" (Mt 10:34).[74] Jesus told us, "You will indeed
drink the cup that I drink, and with the baptism I am
baptized with you will be baptized" (Mk 10:39).
Persecution is the baptism of fire that the church is to
go through in order to be made white and clean while
she reaches the lost for Christ. Perhaps this is no more
clearly portrayed than in Revelation 12:1-6:

> And a great sign appeared in heaven: a woman
> clothed with the sun, with the moon under her feet,
> and on her head a crown of twelve stars. *She was*
> *pregnant and was crying out in birth pains and the*

---

[73] See Chapter one. Tribulation results when the elect are gathered
by God's Spirit.
[74] Dietrich Bonhoeffer, *The Cost of Discipleship* (New York:
Macmillan, 1963), 243.

agony of giving birth. And another sign appeared in heaven: behold, a great red dragon, with seven heads and ten horns, and on his heads seven diadems. His tail swept down a third of the stars of heaven and cast them to the earth. And the dragon stood before the woman who was about to give birth, so that when she bore her child he might devour it. *She gave birth to a male child, one who is to rule all the nations with a rod of iron, but her child was caught up to God and to his throne, and the woman fled into the wilderness, where she has a place prepared by God, in which she is to be nourished for 1,260 days* [emphasis added].

The woman who is clothed with glory is the messianic community, the bride of God (Is 26; 54; Eph 5:31-32; Rev 22:17; 21:2, 9). And although the mother of Jesus may be secondarily in mind, the woman represents the people of God living both before and after Christ's coming. This is because, after the woman Israel gives birth to the Christ, she is persecuted and flees into the desert having other children who are described as those who keep the commandments of God–Christians (Rev 12:13-17). [75]

The woman's birth pangs in verse two represent the afflictions of the covenant community, and particularly the messianic line, leading up to Christ's birth (Is 26:17-19). The dragon of verse three, represents the devil, who, working his will by means of demonic forces, galvanizes the evil kingdoms of the earth to persecute God's people (Dan 7:21-22; 11:35; Rev 2:10;

---

[75] This woman is the bride of God and of Christ, as the apostle Paul declares "the Jerusalem above is free, which is the mother of us all" (Gal 4:26); and which the prophet Isaiah so frequently refers to (Is 52:2; 54:1-6; 61:10; 62:1-5, 11; 66:7-13, cf. Is 26:16-19).

13:7; 17:3-6). Verse four summarizes all of the devil's efforts to exterminate the Seed of the woman (Gen 3:15); from His birth (Lk 4:28-30), to His ministry and finally at the Cross. And finally, verse five is a clear reference to Christ:

> She bore a male Child who was to rule all nations with a rod of iron. And her Child was caught up to God and His throne (cf. Ps 2:7-9).

Additionally, the seed of the woman is not only Christ but also the covenant community. Greg Beale explains, "The primary purpose of the abbreviation and the portrayal of Christ as a child is to identify him with the wider perspective of the church's historical life."[76] Then, in verse six, the woman is depicted as beginning to experience both the spiritual protection of God as well as tribulation in the world, as she is protected from the dragon for one thousand two hundred and sixty days. This, as we've seen, signifies the period of time between Christ's ascension and second coming; the duration between Christ's inauguration and consummation of His kingdom (Rev 11:2-3; 12:6, 14; 13:5).

What we should clearly see in Revelation 12 is that the conflict between the church and the world is but a manifestation of the war between Christ and the devil. This truth is revealed in Revelation 12:7-12 where Satan is cast out of heaven by Michael and the holy angels. We are not to think of the war in heaven in verse seven as the fall of Satan at the time of creation. What we are to see is the defeat of Satan which

---

[76] Beale, *The Book of Revelation*, 639.

occurred in the crucifixion and resurrection of Jesus Christ. These verses are a narration of the defeat the devil and his angels suffered by Michael and his angels in heavenly combat. Thus, verses 7-12 are the heavenly counterpart to verses 1-6.[77]

The emphasis of Revelation 12 is the spiritual protection of God's people against evil because of Jesus Christ's defeat of Satan and the powers of darkness through His death and resurrection. Armed with this truth, Christians are to courageously persevere in their witness despite persecution. And that is what the song in Rev 12:11 is all about. The saints can be assured that their suffering is not only part of God's plan but also part of Christ's victory (Rev 12:11). The cosmic victory of Christ on earth and of the archangel Michael in heaven is the basis for the victory that suffering Christians on earth win over the devil throughout history.[78]

The Bible likens Satan to a despot who has conquered the whole world, holding mankind hostage as slaves to do his bidding. But the Son of God invades the strong man's occupied territory, and plunders his house (Mt 12:29), setting the captives free (Lk 4:18-19). Satan now wars against the seed of the woman (Rev 12:17) and tribulation is the result. What the

---

[77] The Devil is both the deceiver and the accuser of God's people (Rev 12:9). However, Christ's redemptive work has made it impossible for the Devil to accuse the saints (Rom 8:1, 33-34). And because the devil was cast out of heaven, his charges having become groundless. Thus, Christ's redemptive work not only loosed God's people from the penalty of their sins, but protects them from the damning accusations of the Devil (Job 16:19; Rom 8).

[78] Beale, *The Book of Revelation*, 663.

Apocalypse shows us regarding the nature of tribulation is Satan uses two basic tactics: persecution that comes by way of the state and false teaching and deception from within the church (Dan 11:32-35; Acts 20:29-31; 2 Thess 2:3-4; Rev 13:7). Satan's purpose is to sweep the church away with a deluge of deception, debauchery and dilution (Rev 12:16). Satan's scheme is to infiltrate the church with false teachers to deceive her and compromisers to water-down the gospel to contribute to her downfall and to hold the world in blindness (2 Tim 2:23-26; Rev 2:14-22; 3:15-17).

As noted earlier, covenant loyalty is the target of demonic rage. This is made clear to us in Revelation 12:17 which declares that the dragon who was thrown down by Christ's victory at Golgotha "became furious (ὀργίζω) with the woman and went off to make war on the rest of her offspring, on those who keep the commandments of God and hold to the testimony of Jesus."

An argument put forward here by Dispensationalists is worthy of our attention. The argument envisions the 'saints' of Rev 12:17 to be the believing Jews of the elect 144,000; the so-called tribulational saints rather than Christians.[79] However, the Dispensational understanding of this verse is simply wrong because it makes a distinction between believing Jews and Gentiles which God Himself doesn't make (Rom 10:12). The NT declares that the church consists of both believing Jew and Gentile (Rom 1:16; Gal 3:28; Eph 3:6). Because of Christ's redemptive work of the cross there is thus no longer are any distinctions to be made

---

[79] Robert L. Thomas, *Revelation 8-22: An Exegetical Commentary* (Chicago, IL: Moody Press, 1995), 142.

between believing Jew and Gentile (Acts 15:9). Moreover, the NT equates OT promises which deal exclusively with the restoration of Israel, the Kingdom of God, the work of the Messiah, etc., and applies it to the church (Act 15; 1 Pet 2:9).[80]

Thus, when the apostle Paul declares "And in this way all Israel will be saved," he refers to the completed remnant consisting of believing Jew and Gentile, which in the apostle's present time are being gathered and will continued to be gathered in the interadvent period from "all nations, tribes, peoples, and tongues" (Rom 11:26; Rev 7:9).[81] The future of ethnic Israel is an integral part of the current era of gospel proclamation.[82] God has only one saving program – the church (Mt 16:18). This is not replacement theology. The NT church has not replaced Israel, it is the extension of the OT church (Eph 2:19-3:6). This is why the apostle Paul in Galatians calls NT believers "Abraham's seed" (Gal 3:26-29).

Looking back at Rev 12:17, could it really be said that the term 'saints' in the New Testament can mean anything other than believers in Jesus Christ? This argument could be advanced for the entire Bible (Confession of Faith 8.6; 11.6). It is therefore pure speculation on the part of the Dispensationalist to say

---

[80] The following Old Testament passages referring to Israel are applied to the church in the New Testament: (1) Ex 19:5-6 = 1 Pet 2:9; (2) Jer 24:7 = 2 Cor 6:16; (3) Jer 31:31-34 = Lk 22:20; (4) Lev 19:2 = 1 Pet 1:15; (5) Hos 1:10 = Rom 9:22-26; (6) Hos 2:23 = 1 Pet 2:9-10; (7) Amos 9:11 = Acts 15:16 (there are more).
[81] O. Palmer Robertson, *The Christ of the Covenants* (Phillipsburg, NJ: P&R, 1980), 172, 188-189.
[82] Robertson, *The Israel of God*, 173.

that "the church is never mentioned in any passage relating to the Great Tribulation."[83]

Suffice it to say that according to the Bible, the church, which is the pillar and ground of truth, is the Israel of God (Gal 6:16; 1 Tim 3:15). In summary, it borders on the absurd and convolutes the gospel to make distinctions where God does not.

Tribulation-Kingdom-Endurance

In the Book of Revelation, the apostle John identifies himself with fellow Christians and with Jesus as: "Your brother and fellow partaker" in the tribulation and kingdom and endurance of Jesus Christ (Rev 1:9). In this triad, John and all believers are brothers and fellow partakers of: (1) the *tribulation* – persecution, affliction, distress which comes on account of the gospel witness, and (2) *kingdom* – the exercise of rule in the present and future kingdom of Christ, and (3) *endurance* – the remaining faithful to Christ despite persecution. These three words "the tribulation and kingdom and endurance" mutually interpret one another, in that they have a single article.

By this tribulation-kingdom-endurance paradigm, which we will refer to as the 'conqueror's paradigm,' Christians are exhorted to faithfully endure tribulation and conquer in the power of Christ as they witness the gospel. The appropriateness of this term becomes apparent when one considers the promises of Christ in the Apocalypse such as "he who endures to the end shall be saved," are for the one who conqueror and inherit eternal life (Rev 2:10). Having defined

---

[83] Chafer, *Major Bible Themes*, 325.

tribulation and kingdom in earlier discussions, we move to discuss endurance.

The word endurance, from the Greek ὑπομονή, *hupamane* literally "a remaining," can mean steadfastness, constancy, and patiently enduring. It is a cognate of ὑπομένω *hupameno*, literally, remaining under (the load), bearing up (cf. 1 Thess 3:5). In light of what we've discussed regarding the inaugurated end-time birth pangs of the messianic community, endurance ὑπομονή is equated with intense desire to see a thing come about; "My little children, for whom I labor in birth again until Christ is formed in you" (Gal 4:19).

The connection between endurance and tribulation therefore comes into focus when we consider that ὑπομονή is enduring the unknown despite the fear one feels. For endurance is an attitude of the soul that perseveres in the hope that the Lord of all the earth will do right (Gen 19; Dan 12:12). Thus, believers learn to endure as grace is bred into their souls. As we hope to demonstrate, the conqueror's paradigm forms the eschatological structure of the end times discourses in the rest of the NT.

Tribulation-Kingdom-Endurance in the Gospels

Christ Himself builds His church, and all the powers of darkness cannot overpower it (Mt 16:18). Through the power of Christ, the church pushes back the domain of spiritual death, rescuing redeemed prisoners (Is 49:9, 24-26; Mt 12:29). And because Christ builds His church in the very precincts of the gates of hell, we are to expect nothing less than the utmost hostility and persecution. In the Olivet Discourse, Jesus lays out a picture of the interadvent period:

> And Jesus answered them, see that no one leads you astray. For many will come in my name, saying, "I am the Christ," and they will lead many astray. And you will hear of wars and rumors of wars. See that you are not alarmed, for this must take place, but the end is not yet. For nation will rise against nation, and kingdom against kingdom, and there will be famines and earthquakes in various places. All these are but the beginning of the birth pains. Then they will deliver you up to tribulation and put you to death, and you will be hated by all nations for my name's sake. And then many will fall away and betray one another and hate one another. And many false prophets will arise and lead many astray. And because lawlessness will be increased, the love of many will grow cold. But the one who endures to the end will be saved. And this gospel of the kingdom will be proclaimed throughout the whole world as a testimony to all nations, and then the end will come (Mt 24:4-14).[84]

Jesus gives us the express purpose of preaching–a witness to all nations (Mt 24:14). He said, "They will deliver you up to tribulation and kill you, and you will be hated by all nations for My name's sake." This is the cost of completing the Great Commission (Mt 24:9). As we have seen, the birth pangs mentioned in verse eight represent the afflictions of the covenant

---

[84] The following is my understanding of Matthew 24:1-31: (1) Interadvent period (Mt 24:14-14); (2) AD 70 sign (Mt 24:15-28); (3) Parousia (Mt 24:29-31).

community, who are the targets of demonic rage directed against the saint's obedient lives and faithful witness to Christ's saving power (Rev 1:9; 12:11). This obedience brings tribulation, as believers spiritually fulfill the same office as Christ in this age by following His model, being faithful witnesses (Rev 1:5).

In light of what has been articulated here: (1) tribulation itself affords the saints an opportunity to testify (Mt 24:9; cf. Lk 21:13), (2) to ensure the saints are successful in their testimony, God gives the grace of patient-endurance (Mt 24:13), and (3) God delays His final judgment until the full number is brought in—all Israel is saved (Mt 24:14; Rom 11:25-26).

This leads us to consider our second point: Tribulation serves as the means for hardening and judging the reprobate. As noted, an end-time judgment will occur at the end of history, notwithstanding, sometimes that judgment intrudes into this age. This may come in the form of warnings and prejudgment for non-believers or range from chastening to suffering with Christ for believers. However, the final judgment is delayed, or timed to coincide with, the full number of God's people coming to salvation (Mt 1:21; Rom 11:25-26; 2 Pet 3:9). While the gospel goes out, God gives staying power to His church while the full number comes in, and the very attitude of the church during this time of testing and suffering is important.

Further in the Olivet Discourse we have Christ's description of the end of the world:

> Immediately after the tribulation of those days the sun will be darkened, and the moon will not give its light; the stars will fall from heaven, and the powers

of the heavens will be shaken. Then the sign of the Son of Man will appear in heaven, and then all the tribes of the earth will mourn, and they will see the Son of Man coming on the clouds of heaven with power and great glory. And He will send His angels with a great sound of a trumpet, and they will gather together His elect from the four winds, from one end of heaven to the other (Mt 24:29-31).

As verse 29 clearly declares, Christ will come again (second coming) immediately *after* the tribulation. Accompanying His return will be heavenly portents and cosmic upheaval in the sun, moon and stars. Verse 30 tells us Christ will be seen "coming on the clouds of heaven with great power and great glory." And with the sound of a mighty trumpet, as verse 31 declares, Christ will send forth His angels to gather up the elect (Christians) from the whole earth (1 Cor 15). The fact that this refers to a general resurrection is understood by a parallel passage in Matthew 13:41-43, which tells us the wicked will be *gathered out* of Christ's kingdom (before the elect).

When we turn to the Markan apocalypse in Make 13, we find the conqueror's paradigm with the added assurance that the Holy Spirit Himself will articulate the saints testimony (Mk 13:11). This is similar to the promise we have in Luke that tribulation "will turn out for you as an occasion for testimony" (Lk 21:13). For, Christ declares He Himself will speak through His witness and provide a "mouth and wisdom, which none of your adversaries will be able to withstand or contradict" (Lk 21:15; cf. Is 54:17).

In John's Gospel, we have a different structure altogether. And while it lacks the tribulation-kingdom-endurance paradigm (to my knowledge), a parabolic expression is used and incorporates the main elements of thought. The pericope in question occurs in John, where Jesus says:

> Truly, truly, I say to you, you will weep and lament, but the world will rejoice. You will be sorrowful, but your sorrow will turn into joy. When a woman is giving birth, she has sorrow because her hour has come, but when she has delivered the baby, she no longer remembers the anguish, for joy that a human being has been born into the world. So also you have sorrow now, but I will see you again, and your hearts will rejoice, and no one will take your joy from you (John 16:20-22).

Here we have the familiar end times description of the woman Israel giving birth to the messianic community (Rev 12; cf. Is 26:17-18). This is accompanied by the language of affliction (θλῖψις) which the covenant community suffers for its faithfulness.

Tribulation-Kingdom-Endurance in the Pauline Corpus

As stated earlier, believers may rest assured that Christ indeed bore the wrath of God for our sins so that our sufferings are never punishment from God but a call to suffer with Christ, not to bear our sins, but to love the way He loved and be ready to suffer for doing the will of God the way He did (Phil 2:5-11). And in the Pauline corpus we have at least two main triads: the conqueror's paradigm and the faith-hope-love paradigm. For an example of the first, Paul employs

64

the words tribulation, kingdom, and endurance together in one unique pericope:

> We ought always to give thanks to God for you, brothers, as is right, because your faith is growing abundantly, and the love of every one of you for one another is increasing. Therefore we ourselves boast about you in the churches of God for your steadfastness (ὑπομονῆς) and faith in all your persecutions (διωγμοῖς) and in the afflictions (θλίψεσιν) that you are enduring. This is evidence of the righteous judgment of God, that you may be considered worthy of the kingdom (βασιλείας) of God, for which you are also suffering since indeed God considers it just to repay with affliction (θλῖψιν) those who afflict (θλίβω) you, and to grant relief to you who are afflicted (θλίβω) as well as to us, when the Lord Jesus is revealed from heaven with his mighty angels in flaming fire, inflicting vengeance (ἐκδίκησις) on those who do not know God and on those who do not obey the gospel of our Lord Jesus. They will suffer the punishment of eternal destruction (ὄλεθρος), away from the presence of the Lord and from the glory of his might, when he comes on that day (ἐν τῇ ἡμέρᾳ ἐκείνῃ) to be glorified in his saints, and to be marveled at among all who have believed, because our testimony (μαρτύριον) to you was believed (2 Thess 1:3-10).

In this inaugurated end-times rich pericope, the apostle reminds the Thessalonian believer's that their partaking of Christ's tribulations θλίψεων is not only proof of their election, but proof that God will inflict talionic vengeance ἐκδίκησις upon the wicked for their treatment of them.

Part of God's talionic judgment on those who are afflicting the Thessalonian church is mediated by saintly prayers for justice (Rev 6:10). The unbelieving world, rejecting the gospel and persecuting the saints, incur God's talionic judgment which is mediated by saintly prayers for justice.[85] Despite it all, Paul is grateful that faith is growing and love is increasing (verse 3). For as the apostle declares in 1 Cor 13, love is the indefatigable capacity to endure despite the ingratitude without complaining or becoming discouraged.

The Redemptive Power of Tribulation

Hope enables us to endure, love compels us to labor, albeit bringing tribulation (2 Thess 1:3-10; cf. 1 Thess 1:3). Faith lays hold of the promises of God in Christ and breaks forth in action, but this work of faith brings with it the world's hate. And so tribulation ensues, ushering in its train a progressive pressure and maddening violence which seeks to eradicate the offending witness that brought the threat of destruction. This is the essence of what the apostle Paul teaches us in 2 Corinthians 1:6; four cognates of tribulation are used four times. An amalgamation between the conqueror's paradigm and Paul's faith-hope-love triad may be made as follows:

(1) Tribulation (work of faith)—our faith in Christ and the preaching of the gospel brings tribulation.

---

[85] Johannes G. Vos, "The Ethical Problem of the Imprecatory Psalms" *Westminster Theological Journal* 4 (1942): 124.

(2) Kingdom (labor of love)—our love for our fellow man compels us to tell others about Jesus Christ.

(3) Endurance (patience of hope)—patience defines our character—it's essential to steadfastness.

This leads us to consider our third point: Tribulation afford the saints an opportunity to testify unto the effectual gathering of all the elect. What Paul teaches us in 2 Corinthians 1:6 and in Colossians 1:24 is the sufferings of Christ in His people are a continuation of His ministry. 2 Cor 1:6 tells us "If we are afflicted, it is for your comfort and salvation; and if we are comforted, it is for your comfort, which you experience when you patiently endure the same sufferings that we suffer."

The point is: *Tribulation is the price for winning the lost, as the sufferings of believers extend Christ's afflictions to the people they were meant to save* (Is 53:10-11; 63:9; Col 1:24). This is why the apostle declares "Now I rejoice in my sufferings for your sake, and in my flesh I am filling up what is lacking in Christ's afflictions, that is, tribulations (θλίψεων), for the sake of his body, that is, the church" (Col 1:24). Thus, suffering affords Christians the opportunity to witness the saving power of Christ (2 Cor 4:10-11; Col 1:24-29; 1 Pet 2:19-20).

Let us understand that Paul is not saying that Christ's afflictions are lacking in their atoning efficacy. For they are sufficient for the elect (Mt 26:28). However, Christ's sufferings are unto propitiation (salvation) while Christian sufferings are unto propagation, *viz.*, Christ's sufferings unto the salvation of the elect are made known to others by way of believer's verbal witness, holy life and sufferings (Rev 12:11).

In conclusion, Christian endurance is set in relation to tribulation and kingdom. The church, as brothers and fellow partakers of Christ's kingdom, must continue to endure tribulation while faithfully testifying the gospel until all Israel is saved and then the end will come.

Chapter Four:
The Historical Understanding of Tribulation

"It would be difficult to suppose that God had left His people in ignorance of an essential truth for nineteen centuries."
– George E. Ladd

Old voices often give needed perspective.[86] In our endeavor to arrive at a fully-orbed understanding of God's purpose for tribulation, we would be remiss if we failed to heed the voice of the historic church. In this chapter my method will not be to leverage the fathers of church history to find authority for our position. For in the church our final authority is Holy Scripture. However, as we survey church history for its view of tribulation, we will find that while millennial views varied, up until around 1830, the consensus of the church was post-tribulational. Beginning with the early church fathers (ECFs), our approach will be to examine three NT texts in order to find if possible a consensus regarding the historic church's understanding of tribulation (2 Thess 2:3-8; Rev 3:10; and John 17:15). [87]

---

[86] S. Donald Fortson III and Rollin G. Grams, *Unchanging Witness: The Consistent Christian Teaching on Homosexuality in Scripture and Tradition* (Nashville: B&H Academic, 2016), 27.
[87] It is generally held that the ECF were those fathers of the church who lived after the apostles and before the eighth century.

The Early Church Fathers

The ECFs are a veritable battleground for theological polemics ranging from spiritual gifts to eschatology. As we approach this chapter, we are wise to remember that when disputing Christian doctrines, there are some inherent dangers to quoting the ECFs. This is because much of their writing can be considered vague and therefore amenable to various doctrinal positions. Moreover, we are reminded of the fact that as the views of some ECFs matured, they, for example like Augustine, changed perspectives (*Retractions*). However, while we must take care to analyze what they have left us in writing, it would, as George Ladd has so poignantly observed, "be difficult to suppose that God had left His people in ignorance of an essential truth for nineteen centuries."[88] The so-called essential truth Ladd refers to is the dispensational concept of the rapture, which envisions an escape from tribulation.

Looking to our first NT text, Paul in 2 Thessalonians 2:3-8 corrects an errant eschatological view that the 'Day of the Lord' had already come. As we've argued in chapter one, the 'Day of the Lord' is the OT technical term for the second coming. Paul writes:

> Let no one deceive you in any way. For that day will not come, unless the rebellion comes first, and the man of lawlessness is revealed, the son of destruction, who opposes and exalts himself against every so-called god or object of worship, so that he takes his seat in the temple of God, proclaiming himself to be God. Do you not remember that when

---

[88] George Ladd, *The Blessed Hope* (Grand Rapids, MI: Eerdmans, 1956), 20.

I was still with you I told you these things? And you know what is restraining him now so that he may be revealed in his time. For the mystery of lawlessness is already at work. Only he who now restrains it will do so until he is out of the way. And then the lawless one will be revealed, whom the Lord Jesus will kill with the breath of his mouth and bring to nothing by the appearance of his coming (2 Thess 2:3-8).

Until the 1830s, when men such as Edward Irving and John Darby introduced and popularized the 'rapture theory,' the eschatological consensus of the church (apart from the question of the millennium) was: (1) a great apostasy would befall the church (2 Thess 2:3), (2) the Antichrist would persecute the church during the great tribulation (2 Thess 2:4), and (3) Christ would return at the end of the age to bring the resurrection and the final judgment (2 Thess 2:8).

What is clear from 2 Thessalonians 2:3-8, as Robert Gundry insightfully observes, is "a pretribulational Paul should have written that events in the tribulation will follow the rapture. Instead, he writes that the day of the Lord will follow tribulational events."[89] Counter to Dispensationalists such as John Walvoord, who claim that the ECFs believed in the imminency of the Lord's return, and therefore they believed in pretribulationism, as has been said, though many of

---

[89] Robert Gundry, *The Church and the Tribulation: A Biblical Examination of Posttribulationism* (Grand Rapids, MI: Zondervan, 1973), 119.

the ECFs were premillennial, they were all post-tribulational.[90]

Looking to our first point, the *Didache*, an early church instruction on Christianity, warns about the realities of apostasy in the last days, and exhorts believers to remain faithful:

> When lawlessness increases, they will hate and persecute and betray one another, and then the world-deceiver will appear claiming to be the Son of God, and he will do signs and wonders, and the earth will be delivered into his hands, and he will do iniquitous things that have not been seen since the beginning of the world. Then humankind will enter into the fire of trial, and many will be made to stumble and many will perish; but those who endure in their faith will be saved from under the curse (burning process?) itself" (Didache 16.4-6).

In the Didache we learn a number of important things about the early church. First, it reflects the teaching of the early church about tribulation which was to be a time before the return of Christ that produces purity or apostasy (16.4). As to our second point, this great falling away in the church will precede the coming of the lawless one, the Antichrist, who will be a satanically inspired world leader at the end of this age (16.4-5). And third, in the understanding of the Didache, the evil career of the man of lawlessness will end only with the return of Christ (16.8). Thus, according to the Didache, the expectation of the early

---

[90] John F. Walvoord, *The Rapture Question* (Grand Rapids, MI: Zondervan, 1979), 270.

church was the coming of a great apostasy, the appearance of the Antichrist and then Christ's second coming.

In light of this expectation, Ladd rightly observes, "The purpose of the Didache was to prepare the church for the Great Tribulation," and he adds, "While the author of the Didache emphasized the spirit of expectancy and watchfulness, he expects the church to suffer at the hands of the Antichrist."[91] Over against this view, Dispensationalist John Walvoord states, "Paul is answering this question in effect, No, you are not going to enter that period. The Lord will come for you first."[92] In response, we ask: Hasn't the church experienced tribulation for the past 2,000 years?

Apparently, for Walvoord's school, Paul's promise that believers weren't to 'enter that period' wasn't for the Christians who perished in the first ten persecutions of the early church or for Christians who continue to suffer tribulation today. Such views fail to square with reality.

In fact, it is estimated that more Christians were martyred in the 20th century (approx. 171,000), than in all previous centuries combined.[93] Christians in Indonesia, Nigeria, Iraq, Sudan, as well as other parts of the world, suffer every day at the hands of Islamic extremists. Christians in Iraq are persecuted daily, and tens of thousands have been forced from their homes. The church in Iraq and Iran has been nearly wiped out by persecution. The church in China faces varying

---

[91] Ladd, *The Blessed Hope*, 21.
[92] Walvoord, *The Rapture Question*, 164.
[93] Robert L. Dana, "Shifting Southward: Global Christianity Since 1945," *International Bulletin of Missionary Research* 24, (2000): 50.

degrees of persecution ranging from harassment, imprisonment, and torture. Yet, this doesn't qualify as great tribulation? A question for Walvoord's school would be: How bad does it have to get before things are considered "great" tribulation?

Pretribulationalists believe the great tribulation to be a time of great cruelty: What about the horrific treatment of Christians in non-affluent countries? Isn't that horrific enough? The point is, according to the ECFs, the Antichrist would persecute the church during the great tribulation (2 Thess 2:4). And as we have argued, the great tribulation corresponds to the duration of time between Christ's two advents.

According to Justin Martyr (AD 100-168), only Christ's second coming will put an end to the Antichrist's attack on the church. He writes:

> Two advents of Christ have been announced: the one, in which He is set forth as suffering, inglorious, dishonored, and crucified; but the other, in which He shall come from heaven with glory, when the man of apostasy, who speaks strange things against the Most High, shall venture to do unlawful deeds on the earth against us the Christians.[94]

As has been said earlier, Christ gave His church teaching on tribulation because His intent was for the church to not only survive all tribulation, but to conquer through it.

Likewise, for the Shepherd of Hermas (AD 150), the great tribulation has already begun. In Vision 4:2:6, God is understood to concomitantly shield His own

---

[94] Justin Martyr, *The First Apology of Justin* (Mahwah, NJ: Paulist Press, 1997), 110.

from wrath as He sends forth His plagues on the wicked: "He both turns away His wrath from you, and again He sends forth His plagues upon you that are of doubtful mind." Just as God's covenant people were preserved through wrath and came out only after the final plague had been executed in Egypt (Ex 12:23), in like manner, the church will remain in the world until Christ's second coming.

In this vein, Tertullian (AD 150-220) observed that the circumstances surrounding the tribulation will be such that "the beast Antichrist with his false prophet may wage war on the church of God."[95] Likewise, Cyril of Jerusalem (315-386) observes: "The church declares to you the things concerning Antichrist before they arrive...it is well that, knowing these things, you should make yourself ready beforehand" (Catechetical Lectures, 15, 9). Similarly, Chrysostom (345-407) writes: "the time of Antichrist will be a sign of the coming of Christ." (Homilies on First Thessalonians, 9); Jerome (340-420) writes: "I told you that Christ would not come unless Antichrist had come before" (Epistle 21); and Augustine (354-430), commenting on Daniel 12, observes:

> But he who reads this passage, <u>even half asleep</u>, cannot fail to see that the kingdom of Antichrist shall fiercely, though for a short time, assail the church before the last judgment of God shall introduce the eternal reign of the saints."[96]

---

[95] Tertullian, *On the Resurrection of the Flesh* (Grand Rapids, MI: Eerdmans, 1997), 563.
[96] Augustine, *The City of God* (New York: Modern Library, 1993), XX, 23, 748.

Returning to one of our earlier themes, according to the early church, the tribulation of the saints in this present age was also understood as the protracted death of Jesus Christ, that is, tribulation is a means for God to demonstrate the grace of Christ (Col 1:24). In this vein, Hippolytus writes:

> If the martyrs, the one who shed their own blood for Christ, were requested to be patient and wait for a while, why cannot you too wait in patience, so that people would be saved and the number of the called and the saints would be completed?[97]

Similarly, Eusebius of Caesarea (263-339), writing of Sanctus, one of the martyrs of the persecution in Lyons AD 177, observes: "Christ suffering in him exhibited wonders; defeating the adversary, and presented a kind of model to the rest." And of all the martyrs, Eusebius adds, "They received their sentence of death with gladness and sang hymns of praise until their last breath."[98]

In sum, far from LaHaye's opinion that the church would not survive tribulation, she has. And for the last 2,000 years, through the power and wisdom of the Holy Spirit, she has not only resisted each successive wave of heresy, by rejecting error and confirming truth, but has withstood each vicious assault of persecution, standing as a rock against which the world has pulverized itself.

---

[97] W. Brian Shelton, *Martyrdom from Exegesis in Hippolytus: An Early Church Presbyter's Commentary on Daniel* (Eugene, OR: Wipf & Stock, 2008), 107.

[98] Eusebius Pamphilus, *Ecclesiastical History* (Grand Rapids, MI: Baker, 1993), 173, 328.

In light of this analysis, regarding the eschatological views of the ECFs, one of the salient points would be the belief in a post-tribulational second coming of Jesus Christ. For while many of the ECFs held to a premillennial view, they were not, however, dispensationalists, but rather believed and taught that the church is the fulfillment of the new covenant declared in Jeremiah 31:31.[99] For example, in his *Dialogue with Trypho*, in response to Trypho's question: "What, then? Are you Israel?" Justin Martyr responds:

> Christ, who begat us unto God, like Jacob, and Israel, and Judah, and Joseph, and David, are called and are the true sons of God, and keep the commandments of Christ (cf. Rev 12:17).[100]

In other words, Justin Martyr replies, "yes." Antithetically opposed to this line of thinking, dispensationalist Robert Saucy comments that statements like Justin Martyr's represent "the capstone of a developing tendency in the church to appropriate to itself the attributes and prerogatives that formerly belonged to historical Israel."[101] Saucy goes on to say, "With Justin's statement, the developing theology of replacement was complete. There was no longer any place for historical Israel in salvation history. The

---

[99] John H. Gerstner, *Wrongly Dividing the Word of Truth: A Critique of Dispensationalism* (Morgan, PA: Soli Deo Gloria, 2000), 3.

[100] Justin Martyr, *Dialogue with Trypho* (Cambridge: MacMillan, 1846), 261.

[101] Robert L. Saucy, *The Case for Progressive Dispensationalism: The Interface Between Dispensational and Non-Dispensational Theology* (Grand Rapids: Zondervan, 1993), 212.

prophecies addressed to this people henceforth belonged to the church."[102]

In response, as the New Testament teaches us, the NT church has not replaced Israel, it is the extension of the OT church (Eph 2:19-3:6). We would add, as Paul makes clear in Romans 9:24-26 ("even us whom he has called, not from the Jews only but also from the Gentiles"), the spiritual fulfillment of Hosea 1:10 and 2:23 is the church. As to the question: What about Israel? *We reply by affirming that the salvation of everyone, regardless of race, is found in none other than Christ and His blood of the new covenant.* And as George Ladd rightly observes, salvation is thus found nowhere else than the "covenant Christ has already established with the church, not through a rebuilt Jewish temple with a revival of the Mosaic sacrificial system."[103] It seems a sober reading of the Book of Galatians would clear all this up.

In sum, along with George Ladd, our conclusion is there is no trace of pretribulationism is the early church.[104] The almost unanimous consensus of the ECFs is a belief that a great apostasy would befall the church in the later days in which the Antichrist would persecute the church. And this time of great tribulation would end only with the return of Jesus Christ (2 Thess 2:3-8).

According to the ECFs, tribulation is to be the church's lot until Christ's return. We now pass over the medieval era and go on to the Reformation. This is for two reasons, want of space, and because in my

---

[102] Ibid.
[103] Saucy, 28.
[104] Ladd, *The Blessed Hope*, 30.

estimation, the next significant development in eschatology occurred at the Reformation.

The Reformation to the Puritans

We are reminded of the spiritual paucity of the age just prior to the Reformation. Out of this Dark Age, the church, experienced the revitalizing voice of God speaking in His Holy Word as the gospel was rediscovered. For in the Reformation, those troubled souls saw the light of the gospel which had been glossed over by centuries old layers of works-righteousness, Mariolatry, the worship of angels, and a plethora of additional assorted old myths. "And yet," as Iain Murray observes, "it must be said that the Reformation period, save for restoring the certain hope of Christ's second coming, did not establish for Protestantism a commonly accepted view of the unfulfilled prophecies which are to precede that coming."[105]

However, it may be said that none of the Reformers (Luther, Calvin, or Zwingli) or evangelical churchmen like John Wycliffe, John Knox, Thomas Goodwin, John Owen, John Wesley, George Whitfield, or Charles Spurgeon ever preached a pretribulation rapture. These Reformers, preachers and theologians studied the Bible most of their lives and never found it anywhere in the Scriptures. What they did find, like the ECFs, was that tribulation is the common lot of the church militant (Rev 3:7). In the time of the Reformation, as Daniel Neil observes, Christians were

---

[105] Iain H. Murray, *The Puritan Hope: Revival and the Interpretation of Prophecy* (Carlisle, PA: Banner of Truth, 2009), 39.

no strangers to persecution: "The light of the gospel broke out again at the Reformation; but, alas! What obstructions has it met with ever since! How much blood has been spilt, and how many families ruined, and sent into banishment, for the profession of it![106]

Another salient facet of Reformation Christianity was the identification of the Pope as the Antichrist. This was the consensus of the Reformers and, to my knowledge all early evangelical churchmen as verified by the Westminster Confession of Faith 25.6:

> There is no other head of the church but the Lord Jesus Christ: nor can the Pope of Rome, in any sense be the head thereof; but is that Antichrist, that man of sin and son of perdition, that exalteth himself in the church against Christ, and all that is called God (25.6).

Further, over against the view that envisions the Antichrist as taking his seat in a rebuilt temple in Jerusalem, we agree with Thomas Manton (and the Puritans) and understand this temple of God to be the church (1 Cor 3:16-17).[107]

In our second text, Revelation 3:10, Christ's promise to the church at Philadelphia is: "Because you have kept My command to persevere, I also will keep you from the hour of trial τηρήσω ἐκ τῆς ὥρας τοῦ πειρασμοῦ which shall come upon the whole world, to test those who dwell on the earth." While this promise offers the church militant Christ's preserving grace in

---

[106] Daniel Neil, *The History of the Puritans* (London: Paternoster, 1822), 21.

[107] Thomas Smith, *The Works of Thomas Manton*, Vol. 3 (London: James Nisbet, 1871), 40.

tribulation, incredibly, dispensationalists find Jesus telling this first-century church that He is going to protect them from a trial that is to take place sometime thousands of years later.[108]

However, Christ's promise is not to remove believers from the realm of evil but protect them in it. Why? Because the church is God's instrument for conveying the message of salvation to the whole world (Mt 24:14).

We find Revelation 3:10's grammatical parallel of τηρήσω ἐκ in Christ's High Priestly prayer in John 17 where Jesus prays to the Father: "I do not pray that You should take them out of the world, but that You should keep them from the evil one τηρήσῃς αὐτοὺς ἐκ τοῦ πονηροῦ." (Jn 17:15). The Great Commission will be fulfilled by no one else but the church. And when all the nations have heard the testimony of the gospel, then the end will come. This was the consensus (to my knowledge) among all the Puritans.

This is, after all, the lesson we have from God's OT church: they weren't removed from Egypt until after the last plague. However, in wrath God remembers mercy, and while He plagued Egypt, He protected His people. The blood-smeared dwelling shielded God's own from the destroying angel (Ex 12).[109] The point is, Jesus doesn't take us out of the storm, He shelters us through it. A particular picture we have of spiritual protection in the midst wrath is that of Revelation 9: While demonic hordes come from the abyss to afflict

---

[108] Hank Hanegraaff, *The Apocalypse Code* (Nashville, TN: Thomas Nelson, 2007), 92.

[109] Meredith G. Kline, *God, Heaven and Har Magedon: A Covenantal Tale of Cosmos and Telos* (Eugene, OR: Wipf & Stock, 2006), 8.

mankind, they are told to afflict only those without the mark of God on their foreheads (Ezek 9; Rev 7). Those marked with God's seal consist of all the elect of all time which is symbolically represented by the 144,000. They are those "who were redeemed from the earth," and consist of "a great multitude which no one could number, of all nations, tribes, peoples, and tongues" (Rev 7:9; 14:1-13).

What Christ promises in Revelation 3:10 is spiritual protection through tribulation, not exemption from tribulation. In other words, Jesus denies a physical removal from tribulation but affirms a spiritual protection from wrath (Jn 17:15). There is no promise in Revelation that God's people shall escape suffering and death, but there is the promise that no harm can come to their souls. It would make no sense for John to tell us that we won't experience tribulation when many had already been slaughtered for their faith. No. The Puritan consensus was the promise to be spared from God's wrath which is far worse than any persecution.

The Modern Church

The bulk of my comments regarding the modern church's understanding of tribulation is reserved for the next chapter. As we've noted before, within the last 150 years the dispensational view of the end times has become the most prevalent. But, as has been seen, Dispensationalism is a novelty that is discontinuous with what the church has believed and taught for twenty centuries. John N. Darby (1800-1882), a Plymouth Brethren, considered the father of modern Dispensationalism, taught a premillennialism that "swept away what had been previously axiomatic in Christian theology."[110] Having invented the doctrines of the secret pretribulational return of Christ and the two saving programs of Israel and the church, Darby then brought his teachings to the United States in the mid-1800s and sold it to many evangelical leaders such as Dwight L. Moody, a popular American evangelist, and Cyrus Scofield, who joined Moody and created a reference Bible which popularized Darby's theology.

As Dispensationalism began to take root in America, Lewis Sperry Chafer, who was discipled by Scofield, started Dallas Theological Seminary (DTS), one of the most influential dispensational evangelical seminaries. Darby's brand of eschatology was further popularized through prophecy charts and authors such as Hal Lindsey, who attended DTS and wrote the Late, *Great Planet Earth* in 1970, and Tim LaHaye, a minister who co-authored the very successful *Left Behind* series of fictional books.

With book sales in the tens of millions, these authors disseminated on a grand scale Darby's eschatology into mainstream Christianity. And today, many preach the dispensational view of the rapture as if it were an established dogma. But few believers today realize that the teaching of Lewis Chafer came from Scofield, who in turn got it through the writings of Darby, who got it from Edward Irving, who himself got it from a Jesuit priest named Immanuel Lacunza.

In sum, how can glibly talk of being removed from tribulation when the pages of church history are blood-spattered with accounts of martyrs and persecutions? For God to rapture His church out of this world in order

---

[110] Murray, *The Puritan Hope*, 210.

to keep her from tribulation would be an affront to the honor and integrity of our bloodstained forefathers. *The church has to be present in tribulation because she is God's mechanism for testifying* (Mt 24:9-14). It is to this line of thinking we now turn.

Chapter Five:
The Theology of Tribulation

"O Sovereign Lord, holy and true, how long before you will judge and avenge our blood on those who dwell on the earth" (Rev 6:10)?

Errant theology hamstrings missions. Consider the account of William Carey, an English Baptist pastor, who was appalled at the indifference the church of his day had for reaching the lost. In Carey's time, a prevalent belief was that the Great Commission was merely for the apostles. When Carey suggested it was the duty of all Christians to spread the gospel, he was told, "Young man, when God is pleased to convert the heathen, He will do it Himself."[111] Many in the church of Carey's day, such as hyper-Calvinists, looked on such efforts as an interference with God's sovereignty; a "profane outstretching of the hand to help the ark of God." Carey rightly argued the Great Commission is the mandate for "all" believers to evangelize the world. This is the church's mandate until the end comes at Christ's second coming (Mt 28:18-20). The Great Commission is not yet fulfilled.

Cultural Withdrawal vs. Cultural Engagement

One of the perennial questions for the church has been: How are we to relate to the world we are called to evangelize? While errant theology hamstrings

---

[111] James Culross, *William Carey* (London: Hodder & Stoughton, 1881), 39.

missions, errant eschatology inherently leads to expressions like: "We should be living like people who don't expect to be around much longer,"[112] so we shouldn't "polish brass on a sinking ship," (J. V. McGee) or "God sent us to be fishers of men, not to clean up the fish bowl" (Hal Lindsey). However, God calls believers to fully engage their culture by "exposing the works of darkness" (Eph 5:11) and bringing "every thought captive to the obedience of Christ" (2 Cor 10:4-5). God commands us to seek the welfare of the culture He has placed us in, "for in its peace we will find (our) peace" (Jer 29:7). For, according to the NT, Christians are elect exiles who are to win souls for Christ (1 Pet 1:2; 2:11-13, 19-20).

We couldn't agree more with Charles Spurgeon who once observed that ideas such as these have:

> Greatly damped the zeal of the church for missions, and the sooner it is shown to be unscriptural the better for the cause of God. It neither consorts with prophesy, honors God, nor inspires the church with ardor. Far hence be it driven.[113]

According to the Bible, Christ has called the church to faithfully proclaim the gospel and live according to biblical standards calling upon men and women of all nations to repent and believe in Jesus Christ, ushering in Christ's lordship not only in their individual lives,

---

[112] Hal Lindsey, *The Late Great Planet Earth* (Grand Rapids, MI: Zondervan, 1970), 145.
[113] Charles Spurgeon, *The Treasury of David: An Expository and Devotional Commentary on the Psalms*, vol 4 (Grand Rapids, MI: Guardian Press, 1976), 102.

but in their families, and societies as well (Mt 28:18-20). A question we might ask in light of our earlier discussions is: Does Matthew 24:14, "And this gospel of the kingdom will be preached in all the world as a witness to all the nations, and then the end will come," refer to the present mission of the church or someone else?

In the dispensational interpretation of Matthew 24:8-14, Jesus is foretelling a period of world evangelization which is to be accomplished by converted Jews of the nation of Israel after the rapture of the church.[114] This particular interpretation has serious ramifications for world missions. Commenting on this Don Fanning writes:

> It becomes a convenient answer to the presumed failure of the church to accomplish the Great Commission as Jesus defined it, but God's will is not limited by or determined by the inability or disbelief of the believers during the Church Age. God will always accomplish His will however long it may take. However, such a post-rapture interpretation of Matthew 24:14 does not infuse a sense of urgency into the mind-set of believers awaiting the return of Christ. *In fact, it quenches the entire focus for completing the Great Commission. It becomes a "self-fulfilling prophecy" of failure. One wonders how prevalent this escapist mentality is* [emphasis added].[115]

---

[114] J. Dwight Pentecost, *Thy Kingdom Come: Tracing God's Kingdom Program and Covenant Promises Throughout History* (Grand Rapids, MI: Kregel, 1995), 251-252.
[115] Don Fanning, "Themes of Theology that Impacts Missions," *Eschatology and Missions* vol. 8(2009): 8.

Moreover, Jesus isn't saying the whole world must be saved before He can return, He says the gospel must be preached to every "nation" ἔθνος (race, people, nation), *viz.*, "nations, tribes, peoples, and tongues," and then the end will come (Mt 24:14; cf. Rev 7:9). This 'end' is not the end of the so-called church age but the end of the world–the Day of the Lord (Is 66:15-16; 2 Pet 3:10).

The point being made here is: One's eschatology drives, or at least affects in large measure, one's evangelical beliefs and efforts. As we have argued, the rapture theory should be jettisoned from the teaching of the church, as such eschatology leaves God's people unprepared for trials and, for the most part, socially irresponsible.

Take for example, the Great Disappointment of 1844. This was a movement in reaction to the teaching of William Miller (1782-1849), a lay Baptist preacher, who, according to his calculations of Daniel 8:14, falsely predicted Christ's second coming. Initially, Miller predicted Christ would return to earth sometime between March 21, 1843 and March 21, 1844. But when that failed to materialize, adjusting his calculation, Miller fixed the new date to October 23, 1844. In response to Miller's preaching, which called for 'true believers' to leave the established church so as not to miss the rapture, thousands left their churches, quit their jobs and gave away their possessions. According to George Knight, there were between 300,000 and a million "Second Adventists" eagerly awaiting Christ's immediate return.[116] But when the prophecy failed to

---

[116] George R. Knight, *Millennial Fever* (Boise: Pacific Press, 1993), 213.

be true, many who had abandoned their worldly possessions became destitute.

In the aftermath, many fell away from Christianity while some returned to their former congregations.[117] Ted Noel, commenting on this episode of church history writes:

> The secret rapture doctrine has the same potential to destroy lives as the Millerite error. It teaches that the church will be removed from the earth before tribulation comes. This promises an easy life for wealthy Christians. They do not have to worry about hardship, since God will protect them from it! And they are just as deceived as the Second Adventists.[118]

What should be quite obvious at this point is: Errant eschatology fails to prepare believers for the trials ahead. For example, in 1974, Corrie Ten Boom, a survivor of a Nazi concentration camp, wrote a letter to the whole church demonstrating the negative effects of the rapture false teaching:

> There are some among us teaching there will be no tribulation, that Christians will be able to escape all this. These are the false teachers that Jesus was warning us to expect in the latter days. Most of them have little knowledge of what is already going on across the world. I have been in countries where the saints are already suffering terrible persecution. In China, the Christians were told, "Don't worry, before

---

[117] Others, unable to admit the failure of Miller's prophecy, recast it as Christ's invisible return, becoming the basis for the Seventh Day Adventist movement.
[118] Ted Noel, *I Want to Be Left Behind* (Maitland, FL: Bible Only Press, 2002), 206.

the tribulation comes you will be translated–raptured." Then came a terrible persecution. Millions of Christians were tortured to death. Later I heard a Bishop from China say, sadly, "We have failed. We should have made the people strong for persecution, rather than telling them Jesus would come first. Tell the people how to be strong in times of persecution, how to stand when the tribulation comes, to stand and not faint."... In the coming persecution we must be ready to help each other and encourage each other... I know that to all who overcome, He shall give the crown of life. Hallelujah![119]

Errant eschatology also causes the church to fall short in its evangelistic efforts. Take for instance the recent ruling of the Vatican which declared that Jews can be eternally saved without the gospel![120] Similarly, some Christian Zionists like John Hagee, teach a dual covenantalism, which understands that Gentiles are saved by Jesus Christ and Jews are saved by law keeping.[121] Now that is replacement theology. Hagee goes as far to say that the Jews never rejected Jesus as the Messiah, but wanted Him to be their Messiah but

---

[119] David Pawson, *When Jesus Returns* (Traveler's Rest, SC: True Potential, 2008), 199.

[120] Kurt Koch, "Commission for Religious Relations with the Jews" available   from http://www.vatican.va/roman_curia/pontifical_councils/chrstuni/relations-jews-docs/rc_pc_chrstuni_doc_20151210_ebraismo-nostra-aetate_en.html; Internet; accessed 14 July 2016.

[121] John Hagee, *In Defense of Israel: The Bible's Mandate for Supporting the Jewish State* (Lake Mary, FL: Front Line, 2007), 133.

Jesus refused. In a video promotion of his book *In Defense of Israel*, Hagee makes the comment:

> In Defense of Israel will shake Christian theology. It scripturally proves that the Jewish people as a whole did not reject Jesus as Messiah. *It will also prove that Jesus did not come to earth to be the Messiah.* It will prove that there was a Calvary conspiracy between Rome, the high priest, and Herod *to execute Jesus as an insurrectionist too dangerous to live. Since Jesus refused by word and deed to claim to be the Messiah, how can the Jews be blamed for rejecting what was never offered?*[122]

And in his book *Should Christians Support Israel?* Hagee goes as far to say, "Let us put an end to this Christian chatter that 'all the Jews are lost' and can't be in the will of God until they convert to Christianity."[123] However, Paul teaches in Galatians 1:9, "If anyone is preaching to you a gospel contrary to the one you received, let him be accursed." In fact, Hagee, who heads the organization *Christians United for Israel*, is more interested in "returning Jewish pilgrims to the land," notes Hank Hanegraaff, "than in turning Jewish people to the Lord."[124] And through the influence of Hagee, and those like him, many believers espouse errant views such as these, and equate a defense of the state of Israel as a test of orthodoxy.

---

[122] John Hagee, "In Defense of Israel" available from https://www.youtube.com/watch?v=tFv5ijz6s6A; accessed 14 July 2016 [emphasis added].
[123] John Hagee, *Should Christians Support Israel?* (San Antonio, TX: Dominion, 1987), 63.
[124] Hanegraaff, *The Apocalypse Code*, 180.

With such a misguided focus, many teach that Israel is the focus of the whole Bible rather than Jesus, and raise millions in support of Israel while homeless Americans live destitute. A good question for Hagee would be: What about Palestinian Christians who are terrorized by Zionists? Or Christians in Jerusalem who are persecuted by Jews? It seems fair to say, the motivation behind such unconditional support is to hasten Armageddon and the end of days. For example, at an inaugural event for Christians United for Israel in 2006, Hagee stated:

> The United States must join Israel in a pre-emptive military strike against Iran to fulfill God's plan for both Israel and the West.... a biblically prophesied end-time confrontation with Iran, which will lead to the Rapture, Tribulation, and the second coming of Christ.[125]

The point is, errant eschatology hamstrings evangelism and missions, and misuses God's resources. One's eschatological views affect one's evangelism.

What we are witnessing in America today is a disintegration of society's foundations, a near complete inversion of values. Now is not the time to disengage with our society and misappropriate millions for misguided schemes in an attempt to pre-empt a so-called pretribulational rapture. God has called the church to transform culture according to biblical standards.

---

[125] Sarah Posner, "Pastor Strange Love" available from http://prospect.org/article/pastor-strangelove; Internet; accessed 14 July 2016.

According to Darby the world is irrevocable. Following suit, today's pre-tribulation rapture theology leads to pessimism toward engagement with one's culture, it discourages believers from becoming involved in science, politics, and business, and it dismisses missions, and minimizes the importance of the visible church.[126]

We might ask: Would the Christian politician William Wilberforce had labored so hard to abolish slavery from his native country of the United Kingdom if he had adopted such a pessimistic view? Or would have William Booth (founder of the Salvation Army) worked so hard to relieve the suffering of the poor? The Christian life is all about balance. As has been said, God would have us be *in* the world, so as to win the lost for Christ. The church must therefore continue to endure all tribulation until all Israel is saved and then the end will come (Mt 24:14; Rom 11:25-26).

Tribulation as a Means for Cultural Engagement

What we have tried to make clear is the church doesn't just fulfill her biblical mandate until the great tribulation begins, because the great tribulation has already begun with Christ's ascension (Rev 12:13). We have argued that God has a purpose for tribulation which not only purifies and strengthens His church, but affords her an opportunity to testify unto the salvation of many (Mt 26:28). Having considered

---

[126] Grayson Carter, *Anglican Evangelicals: Protestant Secessions from the Via Media, c. 1800-1850* (Eugene, OR: Wipf & Stock, 2001), 227.

these things, as well as the manner in which one's eschatology can negatively affect evangelism, we now move to consider how tribulation is a means for believers to fulfill God's purpose in the Great Commission (Mt 28:18-20; cf. Mt 24:9-14).

As we minister in the kingdom of God, we are compelled by the love of Christ to witness to His saving power, which brings the world's hatred and tribulation. However, in God's providential design, tribulation affords a means for: (1) purifying imitation; (2) priestly intercession; (3) and petitioning imprecation. These are three aspects of how the church *embodies Christ's reign* (Rev 20:4).[127] The remainder of this chapter will be an effort to flesh out these concepts.

Purifying Imitation

It has been said, the imitation of Christ is the essence of Christianity. Additionally, as Christians we glorify God by keeping His commandments (Jn 15:8-10), joyfully living out Christ's righteousness (Gal 2:20; Col 3:4), while serving others; allowing our conduct to be directed by the Spirit (Gal 5:25). When saying "imitation of Christ," we mean to say being like Jesus in thought, word, and deed. This is the first way believers embody Christ's reign. This seems to be the express purpose of Jesus when He said, "Follow Me" (Mt 4:19; cf. 1 Cor 11:1; Eph 5:1). And as we've observed in earlier discussions, suffering for Christ is a means of grace.

---

[127] This may be understood in two ways: saints in heaven (the church triumphant), and saints on earth (the church militant).

In the Sermon on the Mount Jesus says, "Blessed are those who are persecuted for righteousness' sake, for theirs is the kingdom of heaven." This eighth Beatitude, relates the truth that sufferings and persecution for the sake of Christ is the inevitable result for those who obey the gospel (Mt 5:10-13). In stark contrast to the prosperity gospel, Jesus says the more you are like Me, the more the world will hate you and persecute you, but the more you will be blessed and will glorify your heavenly Father. Regarding Christian suffering, Thomas Watson writes:

> God has never promised us a charter of exemption from trouble, but he has promised to be with us in trouble. *No vessel can be made of gold without fire; so it is impossible that we can be made vessels of honor, unless we are melted and refined in the furnace of affliction.* God's chastening rod draws Christ's image more distinctly upon us. It is good for there to be symmetry between the Head and the members: to be part of Christ's body; "He was a man of sorrows, acquainted with grief." Hence, it is good to be like Christ, albeit by sufferings [emphasis added].[128]

Importantly, as we've said, Christ has already bore the punishment for our sins so that our sufferings are never punishment from God but a call to suffer with Christ. So, our call to suffer for Christ is not to bear our sins, but to love the way He loved, and to be ready to suffer for doing the will of God the way He did (Mt 20:28; Phil 2:5-11; 1 Pet 4:17-19; Rev 1:9).

---

[128] John A. Dey, *Puritan Gems: or Wise and Holy Sayings of the Rev. Thomas Watson* (London: Paternoster, 1850), 2-9.

Suffering for Christ is a means of grace (1 Pet 2:19-25). As the author of Hebrews reminds us, believer's sufferings are tokens of God's fatherly love and care. Those adopted into Christ's household must endure God's Fatherly chastening (Heb 12:7-8), while others prove they are not God's own by departing (Mt 13:19-22; 1 Jn 2:19). This is part and parcel of God's refining work in the life of one He has regenerated and called to live within His covenant community. God's refining process is so that His Son will be more clearly displayed in us (1 Cor 11:1; Eph 5:1).

Tribulation scatters God's people like seed (Acts 8:1). As Bonhoeffer observes, "God's people must live in distant lands among unbelievers, but they will be the seed of the kingdom of God in the world."[129] Surely this is what Christ means when He says, "Unless a grain of wheat falls into the ground and dies, it remains alone; but if it dies, it produces much grain" (Jn 12:24). In this vein, Thomas à Kempis writes, "Thy afflictions have taught me and all believers that tribulation is the passage to Thy heavenly kingdom, and that the proper method of attaining Thy crown is being made a partaker of Thy cross."[130]

Priestly Intercession

The tribulation that purifies the church also opens the way for the gospel (Acts 8:1). The second way

---

[129] Dietrich Bonhoeffer, *Life Together* (New York: Harper & Row, 1954), 28.
[130] Thomas à Kempis, *The Imitation of Christ* (London: Routledge and Sons, 1888), 162.

believers embody Christ's reign is by their service as ministering priests (1 Pet 2:5). Believers minister as mediating priests by proclaiming God's saving truth (Is 61:6), and extending His tabernacling presence throughout the whole earth through worship, witness, and worthy living (Is 54:2-3; Rev 12:11). By following Christ's model, believers are to faithfully witness by mediating Christ's priestly and royal authority to the world.[131]

Time would fail us to relate how the church has been enabled to do just that. For instance, how John Paton's priestly intercession to the people of the New Hebrides brought whole islands to the feet of Christ; at the cost of his family members. The same could be said of William Carey, Hudson Taylor, Adoniram Judson, Amy Carmichael, Corrie Ten Boom and a long line of saints whose desire to see Christ glorified in the salvation of the elect outweighed thoughts of their own comfort and safety (2 Tim 2:10). After all, it was tribulation that providentially led the early church in Jerusalem to fulfill Christ's gospel mandate (Acts 8:1; 11:19). *God uses tribulation to advance the gospel as the sufferings of believers extend Christ's afflictions to the people they were meant to save* (Col 1:24).

The point is, the love and forgiveness of God is displayed abundantly as believers, who are wronged, hated, and persecuted, extend love and forgiveness to those who have wronged them (2 Cor 5:12-21). It is precisely this priestly intercession in tribulation which affords the church an opportunity to testify and present Christ (Lk 21:7-19; Rom 12:9-21). This is what led

---

[131] Beale, *Revelation*, 193.

Tertullian to say "the blood of the martyrs is seed."[132] Undoubtedly, what Tertullian meant was the willing sacrifice of Christians fertilizes the soil of Christ's Kingdom leading to the conversion of others.

The crux of what we are saying is: Tribulation not only purifies the remnant (all the elect) so that Christ is manifested through the body of the church, but also provides an opportunity for the saints to testify to the forgiveness God offers in the gospel; as well as a practical means of demonstrating the love of Christ. *Thus, tribulation is part of God's plan to reach the lost.* Richard Sibbes, relating the manifold wisdom of God in His use of tribulation unto various ends, observes:

> And mark the extent of the loving wisdom and providence of God, how many things he doth at once. For in the same affliction ofttimes, he corrects some in his children, in the same affliction he tries some grace, in the same affliction he witnesseth to his truth in them, in the same affliction he doth good to others besides the good he doth to them. In the same affliction that others inflict, he hasteneth the ruin of them that offer it; at one time, and in one action, he hasteneth the destruction of the one, by hastening the good of the other; he ripens grace in his children, making them exemplary to others, and all in the same action, so large is the wise providence of God.[133]

As we hope is clear at this point, *God uses tribulation as a providential means of serving His decree of election* (2 Thess 1:5-6). The afflictions that are lacking

---

[132] Tertullian, *Apology*, 50.
[133] Richard Sibbes, *The Works of Richard Sibbes, vol. 3* (Edinburgh: John Grieg and Son, 1862), 107.

of Christ are to be filled up until the whole of His body is gathered.[134] This is why the church cannot be removed from tribulation until the end – the resurrection, the final judgment, and the fiery conflagration which will occur at Christ's second advent. A further facet merits notice. Through the prayers of His saints, God not only delivers His people from their enemies, but works to further purify them while mediating through their prayers His judgment on an obdurate world (Rev 6:10; 8:1-5). It is to this aspect of the saint's mediatory role to which we now turn.

Petitioning Imprecation

God's people are priests who minister-mediate before Him in the true temple to the unbelieving world (Is 54:2-3; Rom 12:1-2; 1 Pet 2:5, 9). The world either receives the saints' mediating witness or rejects it and persecutes them whereby they incur God's talionic judgment which is mediated by saintly prayers for justice (Rev 8:3). This is the third way believers embody Christ's reign – through prayer. Prayer is God's way of stirring up the hearts of His saints, whereby they petition Him for what the Bible categorizes in three ways: (1) protection from wickedness, (2) purifying holiness, and (3) punishing imprecation upon the enemies of God's Kingdom. The thrust of our discussion is to examine this third way God uses prayer.

---

[134] As has been said earlier, Christ's afflictions are not lacking in their atoning value, they are lacking in the sense that not all of His own have come to know of them savingly.

Prayer is an offering up of our needs to God (SCQ 98). We pray to align ourselves with God's will and we pray because God has ordained prayer as one of the means by which He will accomplish His plan (Rev 8:3). When we interact with the transcendent, sovereign, personal, God, our purpose in prayer is not to inform or change His plan in some way but to be a channel through which His ordained plan comes to pass (Ps 141:2; Rev 5:8-11; 6:10; 8:1-5). And the Word of God teaches us, that Christians, responding properly to persecution, are continually called to seek reconciliation and to practice long-suffering, forgiveness, and kindness after the pattern of God (Rom 2:4; Eph 5:1). For the saving power of the gospel is to be ever in view. Accordingly, the Reformer John Calvin writes,

> As we cannot distinguish between the elect and the reprobate, it is our duty to pray for all who trouble us; to desire the salvation of all men; and even to be careful for the welfare of every individual. At the same time, if our hearts are pure and peaceful, this will not prevent us from freely appealing to God's judgment that he may cut off finally the impenitent.[135]

The point is, the saints, viewing trampled justice are to call upon God for vindication and mediate judgment; "And now, Lord, look upon their threats and grant to your servants to continue to speak your word with all boldness, while you stretch out your hand to heal, and signs and wonders are performed through the

---

[135] John L. Thompson, *Reading the Bible with the Dead* (Grand Rapids, MI: Eerdmans, 2007), 66.

name of your holy servant Jesus" (Acts 4:29-30). "But Saul, who was also called Paul, filled with the Holy Spirit, looked intently at him (Elymas the magician) and said, "You son of the devil, you enemy of all righteousness, full of all deceit and villainy, will you not stop making crooked the straight paths of the Lord? And now, behold, the hand of the Lord is upon you, and you will be blind and unable to see the sun for a time" (Acts 13:9-11). "As we have said before, so now I say again: If anyone is preaching to you a gospel contrary to the one you received, let him be accursed" (Gal 1:9). "Alexander the coppersmith did me great harm; the Lord will repay him according to his deeds" (2 Tim 4:14). This is referred to as imprecation. In this vein Richard Belcher notes,

> As the gospel goes forth there is the real possibility of the conversion of God's enemies, not just condemnation or destruction. Both aspects are in view in the phrase of the Lord's Prayer, 'thy kingdom come.' For God's kingdom to come may mean the destruction of God's enemies, but it may also mean the conversion of God's enemies through the preaching of the gospel.[136]

Thus, when God's people pray for deliverance from their enemies, in response to injustice, they are essentially praying for Christ to come and consummate His Kingdom (Mt 6:8-13). By prayers, God not only delivers His people from their enemies, but works to further purify them while mediating through their prayers His judgment on a recalcitrant world. God

---

[136] Richard Belcher, *The Messiah and the Psalms* (Ross-shire: Mentor, 2006), 81.

presses a need upon His people to cry out to Him for sanctifying grace, deliverance, and justice.

By these prayers, God not only delivers His people from their enemies, but works to further purify them, either by malevolent or benevolent agents, while mediating through their prayers His judgment on an obdurate world (Ps 141:6, 10; Rev 6:10; 8:1-5). As the prayers of Christ demonstrate, the days of vengeance are also the days of gathering the elect—the cup of blessing is also the cup of vengeance (Lk 22:20, 42).

No less central to this line of thought is John's vision of the martyrs in Revelation 6:9-11 and 8:1-5. In the vision, incense is offered up with prayer; actualizing both God's preserving presence as well as His talionic judgment on unbelievers. In Revelation 5:8, as John is in the throne room of heaven, where the Lamb will shortly begin opening the seven-sealed scroll and executing God's plan for the ages, we read this:

> And when he had taken the scroll, the four living creatures and the twenty-four elders fell down before the Lamb, each holding a harp, and golden bowls full of incense, which are the prayers of the saints (Rev 5:8).

The prayers of the saints are pictured as incense in the throne room of Heaven, they cry out with a loud voice, "O Sovereign Lord, holy and true, how long before you will judge and avenge our blood on those who dwell on the earth (Rev 6:10)?"

This call for vengeance does not arise from malicious intent, but from a desire to see God's justice vindicated (Ps 37:6; 79:10-12; Is 26:21; 54:17; Rev 11:18). "The saints do not cry out for a personal vendetta," as Joshua

Owens explains, "but for a demonstration of the righteousness of God that restores order to chaos."[137] The basis for the final judgment will therefore correspond to one's relation to Christ. Whether one has experienced saving faith in Him or has rejected God's overtures of love through Him (2 Cor 5:20-21).

Consequently, judgment will reflect the manner in which one has treated Christ by way of His followers, as the parable of the sheep and goats reveals (Ps 69:9; 79:12; Mt 25:31-46, cf. Acts 7:51-53; 9:4); the afflictions of Christ being filled up as the whole body is gathered (2 Cor 1:6; Col 1:24). And as the Apocalypse uncovers, the *lex talionis* is the operative principle of God's justice.

This standard of justice is a warning to those tempted to compromise with the world, and a comfort to those who find no justice from the courts of men. Ironically, because of the principle of equivalent punishment, the persecutors of the church guarantee a death penalty (second death) for themselves by murdering Christ's witnesses. This of course, hangs over their head unless Christ in His grace saves the persecutor – as He did the apostle Paul (1 Cor 15:9). Martyrdom therefore determines the sentence against the persecutors of the church.[138]

---

[137] Joshua Owen, "Martyrdom as an Impetus for Divine Retribution in the Book of Revelation" available from http://digital.library.sbts.edu/handle/10392/479; Internet; accessed 14 July 2016.

[138] Joshua Owen, "Martyrdom as an Impetus for Divine Retribution in the Book of Revelation" available from http://digital.library.sbts.edu/handle/10392/479; Internet; accessed 14 July 2016.

When we come to Revelation 11, we find in the vision of the two witnesses, all three manners in which the church embodies Christ's reign: purifying imitation, priestly intercession, and petitioning imprecation. The two witnesses are not Enoch and Elijah, but rather represent the church of all ages (law and grace), who imitate Christ, live holy lives, and faithfully witness the gospel (Rev 12:11).

In the vision of Revelation 11, the church, at the end of its faithful witness of forty-two months (the time between Christ's first and second advent), is utterly broken, and worn out by evil power (Dan 7:21, 25; 11:32-35; Rev 11:7-10). It appears that the church is utterly destroyed (Rev 11:7-10). And when the power of the holy people has been completely shattered (Dan 12:7), and at the height of the power of evil, it is at that time that the Antichrist will be destroyed by the return of Christ (2 Thess 2:8).

Thus, God delays the final judgment until all Israel is saved. God has heard the prayers of His people and is now acting to judge the world that oppresses believers in order to make the kingdom of this world into the kingdom of the Lord and of his Christ (Ex 3:7; Ps 141:6, 10; Dan 4:17; Rev 16:17-21). Thus, the final reality of a pure Kingdom waits on the eschatological separation (Mt 13:42). It is like how Philip Schaff recounts:

> The long and bloody war of heathen Rome against the church, which is built upon a rock, utterly failed. It began in Rome under Nero, it ended near Rome at

the Milvian Bridge, under Constantine. Aiming to exterminate (the church), it purified (it).[139]

And Christ, breeding endurance into the souls of believers, enables us to persevere, unto the salvation of the elect, through the ministry of Christ in the church (Heb 13:20-21).

---

[139] Philip Schaff, *History of the Christian Church* vol. 3, (Peabody: MA, Hendrickson, 2009), 34.

Chapter Six:
Why Christians Suffer

"We are immortal till our work is done." – George Whitefield

We have made an effort to demonstrate that while believers may suffer tribulation in this life, they will never suffer God's wrath. God has a purpose for suffering. The following are at least ten ways that God uses suffering in the lives of His people:

1. *Suffering is part and parcel of living in a fallen world that is under the sentence of death* (Gen 3:15-24; Rom 5:12-21; 8:18-20). The wrath of God is death and condemnation. We must remember that death signifies God's judgment. D.A. Carson helps us remember this fact when we think we are all entitled to seventy years on this planet. He writes, "For the believer, the time of death becomes far less daunting a factor when seen in the light of eternity...although death remains an enemy, an outrage, a sign of judgment, a reminder of sin, and a formidable opponent, it is, from another perspective, the portal through which we pass to consummated life."[140]

It's important to remember, that as Christians, we have hope even in death because Christ has already conquered Satan, death and hell, and those who are alive in Jesus Christ will never see death but will pass from this life seamlessly into the next (1 Thess 4:15). Death is therefore a defeated enemy that we will face in the confidence that Christ already has the victory

---

[140] D.A. Carson, *How Long, O Lord? : Reflections on Suffering and Evil*, (Grand Rapids: Baker, 2006), 133.

(Jn 11:25-26; 1 Cor 11:25-26; 2 Cor 5:8; Rev 1:5, 18). For the Christian, death is an entrance into glory.

2. *God uses suffering to separate His people from the false contentment of the world* (Dt 8:3; Mt 10:34-37; 13:21). God uses suffering to sever our allegiance and bondage to the world. In order to keep His saints from finding their way in the world, or the world from finding its way in the saint, God employs various trials enabling us to keep our eye on the prize. C.S. Lewis observes, "Prosperity knits a man to the world. He feels that he is finding his place in it, while really it is finding its place in him."[141]

The point is: God doesn't want His saints to grow too comfortable in this world and so He will employ suffering to release our grip on it. For, God has said in His Word, "Do not love the world or the things in the world. If anyone loves the world, the love of the Father is not in him" (1 Jn 2:15).

God desires His people to turn away from the world and look to Him for everything, and He will employ suffering to bring it about. John Piper writes, "For us there is the need, not only to have our obedience tested and proven but also to be purified from all remnants of self-reliance and entanglements with the world."[142] When we suffer trials, God allows us to see how odious sin is and how miserable we are without Him. Describing this further, Richard Sibbes writes:

---

[141] C. S. Lewis, *Screwtape Letters* (New York: Harper One, 1982), 155.
[142] John Piper, *Let the Nations Be Glad* (Grand Rapids: Baker, 2010), 108.

These depths are left to us, to make us more desirous of heaven; else great men, that are compassed about with earthly comforts, alas, with what zeal they could pray, 'Thy kingdom come,' etc.? No; with Peter they would rather say, 'Master, it is good for us to be here,' Mk 9:5; and therefore, it is God's usual dealing with great men, to suffer them to fall into spiritual desertions, to smoke them out of the world, whether they will or not.[143]

3. *God employs suffering as a means of disciplining us so that we will avoid future opportunities to sin.* (Ps 107:17; 119:67, 71; Pro 3:11-12; Heb 12:5-11; Rev 2:9-10). God scourges every son He receives (Heb 12:6). God creates staying power in us so we may endure His chastening love and the world's hate. John Currid rightly sees the suffering associated with God's discipline as preparation. He writes,

> It is like a vaccination for smallpox or some other disease. The inoculation itself is unpleasant, and the side effects are uncomfortable, and the reality is that one is given a minor dose of the disease. However, when confronted with the disease itself, one's immune system is able to fight it because of growing immunity. Thus, one's system is trained and prepared. That is like the Christian life.[144]

God brings temporal judgments upon Christians so that we will not be condemned along with the world (1 Cor 11:32, cf. Rev 2:22). Christ corrects us as He is our

---

[143] Richard Sibbes, Complete Works, VI, 162.
[144] John Currid, *Why Do I Suffer? : Suffering and the Sovereignty of God* (Fearn, Ross-shire: Christian Focus, 2014), 73.

Lord. And this correction shows that we are His legitimate children (Heb 12:11).

4. God ordains suffering so we will rely more on Him and not ourselves (2 Cor 1:9; 12:9; 1 Pet 5:6-7). This is one of the many ways God proves our faith. Afflictions shatter the myth of our self-sufficiency. We clearly see our weaknesses when we suffer. In 2 Corinthians 1:8-9, the apostle Paul tells us, the reason why God appoints sufferings is so that we would not trust in ourselves but in God who raises the dead.

Likewise, John Currid writes, "By means of adversity, God then restores believers to proper creaturely dependence upon Himself. This is to say that God frequently afflicts Christians that they would again realize their hope, joy, and sufficiency lies in Him alone. God is thus being gracious in adversity, and uprooting the Christian from the world."[145]

5. God uses suffering to forge Christ's character in us (Ps 119:66-67, 71; Pro 27:17; Rom 5:1-5; Heb 2:10; 5:8). God's refining process is so that His Son will be more clearly displayed in us. Suffering teaches us that the greatest good of the Christian life is not absence of pain but Christ-likeness. Suffering is one of the means God uses to sanctify us. God's refining process is an expression of his love, never His wrath. His judgment begins with his own people, and then consumes unbelievers (1 Pet 4:17). And only the man who can endure the refining fire of God's holy presence can remain in God's house forever (Jn 8:35).

---

[145] Currid, *Why Do I Suffer?* , 66.

God, as it were, pours Christ's character into us, forming iron in our souls, and works the rough edges out on His anvil of the world (Is 54:16). Thomas Watson insightfully writes,

> God's rod is a pencil to draw Christ's image more lively upon us. It is good that there should be symmetry between the Head and the members. Would we be parts of Christ's mystical body, and not be like Him? His life, as Calvin says, was a series of sufferings, 'a man of sorrows, and acquainted with grief' (Is 53:3). He wept and bled. Was His head crowned with thorns, and do we think to be crowned with roses? It is good to be like Christ, though it be true He drank the poison in the cup (the wrath of God), yet there is some wormwood in the cup left, which the saints must drink: only here is the difference between Christ's sufferings and ours; He were satisfactory (that is, to pay the price for sins), ours are castigatory (that is, in order to amend and correct).[146]

6. *God uses suffering to create in us staying power to faithfully endure persecution* (Jam 1:2-8). God prepares His saints for trouble by causing them to experience suffering. However, this is not just for sufferings sake, but because God's wisdom is as manifold as it is infinite, He causes us to grow in grace, mirroring Christ's image, thereby creating staying power in us, while He prunes us of our sinful proclivities (Jn 15:1-8). The point is: the Christian's continuing (covenant) loyalty to Christ despite trouble

---

[146] Thomas Watson, *All Things for Good* (Carlisle, PA: Banner of Truth, 2009), 28-29.

serves to define our character and produces staying power. When I say staying power I refer to what the Bible calls *patient-endurance.*

Patient-endurance can only be acquired through testing, and suffering definitely tests our faith. For example, the apostle Paul tells us in Rom 5:3-4, "We also glory in tribulations, knowing that tribulation produces perseverance; and perseverance, character; and character, hope." What character is the apostle Paul talking about? The very character of Christ, Who Himself is forming Himself within us. This doesn't mean, of course, that we have only a hope of future joys, we can be full of joy here and now even in our trials and troubles.

Taken in the right spirit these very things will give us patient endurance; this in turn will develop a mature character. A character of this sort produces a steady hope, a hope that will never disappoint us because if we are born again, already we have some experience of the love of God flooding through our hearts by the Holy Spirit given to us. Sufferings temper Christians and is part of God's discipline.

7. *Suffering is the result of a Christian's battle against the three enemies of the kingdom of God – our sin nature, the unbelieving world, and Satan.* When we mortify our flesh, crucify our sin nature, and say no to the desires of the flesh, we carry around in our body the suffering and death of the Lord Jesus (2 Cor 4:11-12). When we take a stand for Christ we will suffer demonic attack and incur the world's enmity, not to mention the fact that our sin nature will hate it, but this will result in the glory of God (1 Pet 4:14).

111

8. *Suffering affords Christians the opportunity to witness the saving power of Christ* (2 Cor 4:10-11; Col 1:24-29; 1 Pet 2:19-20). Suffering furnishes on opportunity for Christians to testify of the saving power of Christ's Cross, and thereby suffer for His sake, for which there will be two ends: a hardening obstinacy for some, and a means of grace for others. God uses Christian suffering to fill up what is lacking in Christ's sufferings (Col 1:24).

Rather than being bitter or upset when justice doesn't come swiftly, we can say along with John Bunyan, "Therefore, I bind these lies and slanderous accusations to my person as an ornament; it belongs to my Christian profession to be vilified, slandered, reproached and reviled, and since all this is nothing but that, as God and my conscience testify, I rejoice in being reproached for Christ's sake."[147]

9. *Suffering affords God the opportunity to manifest His grace.* Tribulation arises on account of the worship of God, the gospel message, and holy living (Rev 12:11). It's important for us to remember that when Job was afflicted he didn't say, the Lord has given and Satan has taken away, no; he said, "The Lord gave, and the Lord has taken away; blessed be the name of the Lord" (Job 1:21). And the Bible, ascribing Job's response as correct says, "In all this Job did not sin *nor charge God with wrong*" (Job 1:22, emphasis added). Job was not suffering for his sins. He suffered so that God might demonstrate that Job would retain his integrity in spite

---

[147] John Bunyan, *The Complete Works, Part IV* (London: Bradley, Garretson & Co, 1873), 69.

of all of his afflictions. Hence, "The greater the trouble, the greater the deliverance."[148]

10. *Suffering is the price for winning the lost for Christ – to fulfill the Great Commission* (Mt 24:9-14). As we have said, Jesus gives us the express purpose of evangelism – to be a witness to all nations (Mt 24:14). The goal of evangelism is for "every tribe and tongue and people and nation" to hear the glorious saving power of Christ's cross; and suffering is the cost of fulfilling the Great Commission. Jesus said, "They will deliver you up to tribulation and kill you, and you will be hated by all nations for My name's sake." This is the cost for the completion of the Great Commission (Mt 24:9).

Likewise, "He who endures to the end shall be saved," is the confidence which a perfect atonement secures (Mt 24:13; Rom 8:28-39). As Christians, we are enabled to do this because we have been crucified with Christ, Who now dwells in our hearts by faith. Christ, Who has rooted and grounded Himself to us in love, compels us to minister the gospel to see the lost saved (2 Cor 5:14; Phil 1:8).

Like Joseph, we may suffer at the hands of even our own family members, but God, working graciously behind the scenes, can bring about a great deliverance out of a great tragedy (Mt 10:34-39). Joseph was a type of Christ; when he suffered, it wasn't because he was a sinner, it was because God was going to use his life to save His people. God takes ordinary people like you and I, and through us accomplishes extraordinary things. God orchestrated events so that the young lad

---

[148] Sibbes, *Complete Works, VI,* 162.

Joseph would end up delivering a nation from certain destruction; Joseph's suffering was the price of it all.

The Bible tells us that Joseph spent roughly thirteen years as either a slave or a prisoner (Gen 37:1; 41:46) but all this was preparing him for extraordinary tasks. And as Joseph's suffering brought about deliverance for others, so does Christian sufferings for the gospel.

It's important to note that, not all suffering seems to fit neatly into one of the above categories we have made. On the Lord's Day, February 6, 1870, the reverend George Mueller's wife Mary died of rheumatic fever. They had been married 39 years. The Lord gave him the strength to preach at her memorial service. He said, "I miss her in numberless ways, and shall miss her yet more and more. But as a child of God, and as a servant of the Lord Jesus, I bow, I am satisfied with the will of my Heavenly Father, I seek by perfect submission to His holy will to glorify Him, and I kiss continually the hand that has thus afflicted me." Suffering doesn't always make sense, but as Christians we have a hope that's beyond death. Our hope is in the One Who has conquered death and lives forever; Who always lives to intercede for us, is preparing a place for us, and will take us to our heavenly home (Heb 7:25).

Delayed Judgment of God

As we noted earlier, an eschatological (end time) judgment will occur at the end of history, notwithstanding, sometimes that judgment intrudes into this age. This may come in the form of warnings and prejudgment for non-believers or range from chastening to suffering with Christ for believers. The final judgment is delayed until the full number of the elect are saved (Mt 1:21; Rom 11:25-26; 2 Pet 3:9).

As we consider how to reconcile the problem of suffering and the goodness and sovereignty of God, we may consider three biblical truths as to why God delays His final judgment: (1) God delays His final judgment until the full number of the elect are saved; (2) God gives staying power to His Church while the full number comes in; and (3) the very attitude of the Church during this time of testing and suffering (the tribulation) is important.

As we look to the first biblical proposition, *God delays His final judgment until the full number of the elect are saved*; let us consider where we would be if, say for instance, Christ's second coming was in the lifetime of our great grandfather, that is before we were born. Where would that put us? We simply would have never existed. For God to have not brought an end to history before you and I were born, and more importantly, before He could reach us with the gospel of Jesus Christ, is a demonstration of His great mercy and patience. As we have said, the first coming of Jesus Christ ushered in the acceptable year of the Lord – that is a space of time for salvation through judgment. The apostle Paul says in 2 Cor 6:2, "Behold, now is the acceptable time; behold, now is the day of salvation."

The Grace of Patience

While this acceptable year lasts, God graciously withholds final judgment, patiently offering full amnesty through the cross of Christ, and suffering occurs because the judgment is delayed until the full number of God's people have come in. The time we currently live in is a day of God's gracious patience. In order for us to fully consider our first premise: *God delays His final judgment until the full number of the elect are saved*, it's important for us to consider the grace of patience.

There are at least eight ways in which we may consider the grace of patience:

1. It is a fruit of the Spirit.
2. It is essential to steadfastness.
3. It can only be acquired through testing.
4. It is given at the appropriate time.
5. It is ultimately what saved the world.
6. It is akin to grace.
7. It is rooted in the wisdom of God.
8. It is the very nature of God.

At the grammatical level, patience in the original Greek is *makrathumia*, which is often translated long-suffering. And is formed from the two words *makras* meaning long or far to denote time and space, and *thumia* which means passion or anger. In the biblical sense it can mean waiting for a sufficient time before expressing our anger while avoiding the premature use of force or retaliation. The words endurance and patience are co-referentially used in Scripture.[149]

F.F. Bruce writes, "If in English we had an adjective 'long-tempered' as a counterpart to 'short-tempered,' then *makrathumia* could be called the quality of being

---

[149] For example, see Lk 8:18; 21:19; Rom 2:7; 5:3-4; 8:25; 15:4-5; 2 Cor 1:6; 6:4; 12:12; Col 1:11; 1 Thess 1;3; 2 Thess 1:4; 3:5; 1 Tim 6:11; 2 Tim 3:10; Tit 2:2; Heb 10:36; 12:1; Jam 1:3-4; 5:11; 2 Pet 1:6; Rev 1:9; 2:2-3; 2:19; 3:10; 13:10; 14:12.

'long-tempered.' Thus, as Bruce says, *makrathumia* is a quality of God.[150] Moreover, endurance is the temper or attitude of the mind that does not easily succumb to sufferings, patience is the self-restraint that does not hastily retaliate a wrong. The one is opposed to cowardice or despondency, the other to wrath or revenge. While endurance is closely allied to hope (1 Thess 1:3), patience is often connected with mercy (Ex 34:6).[151] Thus, we see that endurance is opposed to cowardice and patience to revenge.

1. *Patience is a fruit of the Spirit.* Patience is the fourth of nine communicable attributes of God that are enumerated for us in Gal 5:22. These spiritual fruit proceed from a heart that is made purified in Christ. As the author of Hebrews tells us, we are disciplined by God so that we may be partakers of His holiness, namely patience. This is the peaceable fruit of righteousness that we have been and will be trained by (cf. Heb 12:9-11).

2. *Patience is essential to steadfastness.* Steadfastness is the fruit of patience as patience is the fruit of the Spirit. We cannot endure without the grace of patience, as Jesus declares, "By your patience possess your souls" (Lk 21:19). Throughout the history of the church, what tormenters have resolved to take from Christians is their steadfastness – the staying power of the saints. When they tortured the martyrs, it was their steadfastness they desired to deprive them of. It simply

---

[150] Bruce, *Commentary on Galatians* (Grand Rapids: Eerdmans, 2013), 253.
[151] Lightfoot, *Commentary on Colossians and Philemon* (Peabody: Hendrickson 2008), 67-68.

wasn't enough to take their lives, it goes beyond that. What they hated so much was their ability to endure all that was vented, wanting above all, to hear them beg for their lives, abandoning Christ.

According to the Puritan Thomas Brooks, "Perseverance will make a man hold up and hold on in the work and ways of the Lord, in the face of all impediments, discouragements, temptations, tribulations, and persecutions."[152] Steadfastness ensures that Christians will endure persecution. Satan asked to sift Peter like wheat, but it was Jesus who prayed so that his faith would not fail (Lk 22:31).

3. *Patience can only be acquired through testing.* As we have considered thus far, patience is a grace we receive through testing and suffering. John Bunyan observes, "Temptations, when we meet them at first, are as the lion that roared upon Samson; but if we overcome them, the next time we see them we shall find a nest of honey within them."[153] Again, Bunyan writes, "The Lord uses His flail of tribulation to separate the chaff from the wheat. In times of affliction we commonly meet with the sweetest experiences of the love of God."[154]

We cannot be like Christ except by the testing of our faith. As we have said, God's refining fire is an expression of his love, never His wrath, and only the man who can endure the refining fire of God's holy

---

[152] Thomas Brooks, *Complete Works, Volume 2* (Carlisle, PA: Banner of Truth, 1991) 503.
[153] John Bunyan, *Grace Abounding to the Chief of Sinners* (Carlisle, PA: Banner of Truth, 1991), 2.
[154] Bunyan, *Complete Works,* 79.

presence can remain in God's house forever (Jn 8:35). As J. C. Ryle put it, "The golden Word of God is poured into earthen vessels that undergo fiery preparation."[155]

4. *Patience is given at the appropriate time.* This is our second propositional truth we began with: God gives staying power to His Church while the full number comes in. We need not worry if we can stand up under pressure for God gives patience at just the right time – just when we need it. The Bible tells us so in Luke,

> But before all these things, they will lay their hands on you and persecute you, delivering you up to the synagogues and prisons. You will be brought before kings and rulers for My name's sake. But it will turn out for you as an occasion for testimony. Therefore settle it in your hearts not to meditate beforehand on what you will answer; for I will give you a mouth and wisdom which all your adversaries will not be able to contradict or resist (Lk 21:12-15).

Friends, we have great promises from the Scriptures that the Lord will not abandon us in time of need, but will give us in that very hour the patience that we need. Corrie Ten Boom was a great woman of God who suffered as a Christian under the Nazi regime. During World War II, the Ten Boom home became a refuge, a hiding place, for fugitives and those hunted by the Nazis. By protecting these people, Casper Ten Boom and his daughters, Corrie and Betsie, risked their lives. This non-violent resistance against the Nazi-oppressors was the Ten Booms' way of living out their

---

[155] J. C. Ryle, *Holiness* (Carlisle, PA: Banner of Truth, 2014), 115.

Christian faith. This faith led them to hide Jews, students who refused to cooperate with the Nazis, and members of the Dutch underground resistance movement.

During 1943 and into 1944, the Ten Boom's sheltered seven people in their home. Knowing that the Gestapo could burst into their home at any moment gave the young Corrie much trepidation but not her father. So, Corrie said to her father, "Daddy, I am afraid that I will never be strong enough to be a martyr for Jesus Christ." And her father replied, "'Tell me, when you take a train trip from Harlem to Amsterdam, when do I give you the money for the ticket? Three weeks before?' "'No, Daddy, you give the money for the ticket just before we get on the train.' "'That's right, and so it is with God's strength. Our wise Father in heaven knows when you are going to need things too. Today you do not need the strength to be a martyr; but as soon as you are called upon for the honor of facing death for Jesus, He will supply the strength you need – just in time.'"[156]

Later, the Nazis raided the Ten Boom house and the entire family was arrested and sent to Scheveningen prison. Her two brothers and a cousin were released but her father died ten days later. Then Corrie and Betsie were sent to the Ravensbrück concentration camp in Germany. There Betsie died. As Betsie was dying she said, "We must tell the people what we have learned here. We must tell them that there is no pit so deep that God is not deeper still."[157] The patience needed to say this can only be acquired through testing.

---

[156] Ten Boom, *Tramp for the Lord* (Grand Rapids: Baker, 1974), 125.
[157] Ten Boom, *The Hiding Place* (Grand Rapids: Baker, 2006), 277.

*God gives staying power to His Church while the full
number comes in.*

5. *Patience is what ultimately saved the world.* As
Christians we understand that God's patience has led
to our salvation and will ultimately save a world full of
people that surrender to Jesus Christ. The Puritan
Stephen Charnock, defining divine patience writes:

> It is part of the divine goodness and mercy, yet
> differs from both. God being the greatest goodness,
> hath the greatest mildness. Mildness is always the
> true companion of true goodness, and the great the
> goodness the greater the mildness. Who so holy as
> Christ, and who so meek? God's slowness to anger
> is branch or slip (a means of restraint) from His
> mercy, "The Lord is full of compassion, slow to
> anger" (Ps 145:8). It (divine patience) differs from
> mercy in the formal consideration of the object;
> mercy respects the creature as miserable, patience
> respects the creature as criminal; mercy pities him
> in his misery, and patience bears with the sin which
> engendered that misery, and is giving birth to more.
> Again, mercy is one end of patience; his long-
> suffering is partly to glorifying His grace: so it was in
> Paul (1 Tim 1:16). As slowness to anger springs from
> goodness, so it makes mercy the butt and mark of its
> operations: "He waits that He may be gracious" (Is
> 30:18). Goodness sets God upon the exercise of
> patience, and patience sets many a sinner on
> running into the arms of mercy. That mercy which
> makes God ready to embrace returning sinners,

makes him willing to bear with them in their sins, and wait their return.[158]

Likewise, Arthur Pink observes, "Personally we would define the divine patience as that power of control which God exercises over Himself, causing Him to bear with the wicked and forebear so long in punishing them."[159] God is slow to anger because He is great in power! He has no less power over Himself than He does His creatures (Charnock). This is patience – the power of self-restraint. If we are sinners saved by grace, saved through eternal judgment, saved from eternal destruction then we most certainly understand the ultimate patience that God has manifested in saving us by the blood of His Son Jesus. God's goodness and patience are meant to lead us to repentance (Rom 2:4).

6. *Patience is akin to grace.* The patience we display in suffering can be a means of grace. Suffering affords Christians the opportunity to witness the saving power of Christ. When Christians live righteous lives and suffer for it, the Bible says that it can be a way that God uses to save or further sanctify others (1 Pet 4:19-23). The apostle Peter says it's a gracious thing when we endure sorrows while suffering unjustly (1 Pet 2:19), that is, it's a means of grace, a channel of God's grace for Him to save His people and further sanctify them.

The apologist Justin Martyr, witnessing Christians willing to die rather than recant their faith in Christ,

---

[158] Stephen Charnock, *Discourses Upon the Existence and Attributes of God* (Carlisle, PA: Banner of Truth, 2010), 478-479.
[159] Pink, *The Attributes of God* (Grand Rapids: Baker, 1952), 79.

went from being a follower of Greek philosophers to a follower of Christ. For Justin, the sufferings of Christians was a means a grace. Surely this is what the apostle Paul meant when he said, "I now rejoice in my sufferings for you, and fill up in my flesh what is lacking in the afflictions of Christ, for the sake of His body, which is the church" (Col 1:24).

Christians who live godly lives will most certainly suffer for Christ's sake (2 Tim 3:12). The early Christians rejoiced that they were counted worthy to suffer for the name of Christ (Acts 5:41). When Paul learned that the saints at Philippi were being persecuted he wrote to them, "For to you it has been granted on behalf of Christ, not only to believe in Him, but also to suffer for His sake" (Phil 1:29). In this way, we may understand the expression 'patience is a means of grace.'

Edger Allen Poe once said, "Never to suffer would never to have been blessed." If I may redeem this phrase – never to have suffered for the sake of Christ is to have never been blessed. Isn't this what Jesus means when He says, "Blessed are you when they revile and persecute you, and say all kinds of evil against you falsely for My sake. Rejoice and be exceedingly glad, for great is your reward in heaven, for so they persecuted the prophets who were before you" (Mt 5:11-12)? Suffering is the price for winning the lost for Christ – to fulfill the Great Commission (Mt 24:9-14; 28:18-20).

7. *Patience is rooted in the wisdom of God*. This leads us to our third propositional truth we began with: *the very attitude of the Church during the time of testing and suffering is important*. How we react to suffering

matters, because God demonstrates to the world in the lives of His saints, through both His patience and grace, His mighty power for all who come to Him through His Son Jesus Christ. In us, God manifests His superlative power to save, transform, and keep all who come to Christ in faith. The world is to see Christ in us, as our witness is to point away from ourselves to His power. "For we who live are always being delivered over to death for Jesus' sake, so that the life of Jesus also may be manifested in our mortal flesh" (2 Cor 4:11). "We live as chastened, and yet not killed; as sorrowful, yet always rejoicing" (2 Cor 6:9-10).

How important is our attitude when we are suffering? Peter tells us, it's a gracious thing when we endure sorrows while suffering unjustly" (1 Pet 2:19). Our attitude can be and should be gracious in that they should point us away from what we are suffering at the time, namely to Christ, our heavenly home, and the resurrected glorious bodies we will receive when Christ returns. When suffering comes our way our attitude is very important.

As the Roman poet Lucretius once wrote, "So it is more useful to watch a man in times of peril, and in adversity to discern what kind of man he is; for then at last words of truth are drawn from the depths of his heart, and the mask is torn off, reality remains."[160] The apostle Paul in Romans tells us, "We wait eagerly for adoption as sons, the redemption of our bodies. For in this hope we were saved. Now hope that is seen is not hope. For who hopes for what he sees? But if we hope for what we do not see, we wait for it with patience" (Rom 8:23-25).

---

[160] Lucretius, *On the Nature of Things, Book III*, line 55-58.

This hope is based upon Christ, who is its object. Therefore the hope of the Christian persists in spite of delay and discouraging hardships. It persists in spite of injustice, and lawlessness. As John Calvin observes: "To hope he assigns patience, as it is always conjoined with it, for what we hope for, we in patience wait for."[161] In other words, what we hope for, we patiently wait for. We wait for the resurrection with staying power – the power God supplies, and the continuing (covenant) loyalty to Christ despite persecution serves to define our character and produces patient-endurance by which we may hope large in our inheritance, which is God Himself at the coming resurrection with the personal physical visible return of Christ.

8. *Patience is the very nature of God.* The Bible tells us Christ's sufferings were unto death. They were not momentary. He never begged for His life. He never retaliated in anger. He never sought to punish those who were punishing Him. Instead, those who were inflicting punishment upon Him unjustly He interceded for by saying, "Father, forgive them. For they know not what they do" (Lk 23:34; Is 53:4-12). *God is slow to anger because He is great in power!*

His goodness and patience lead us to repentance. And because Jesus suffered so greatly He is able to comfort so greatly. When you face suffering, Christ will give you His patience that was tested in the fiery trial of Calvary. Our perseverance in suffering is evidence of our saving faith in Christ. We have to be mentally prepared to suffer as Christ suffered, and not retaliate. We must settle this in our minds and entrust our souls

---

[161] John Calvin, *Exposition of Romans 8:24.*

to a faithful Creator while doing good, for what Christ promises is spiritual protection through trials, not exemption from trials (1 Pet 4:19).

Chapter Seven:
Conclusion

"The focus of eschatology and missions is based on the results of one's beliefs about the Second Coming." – Don Fanning

This is no ivory tower debate, as Hank Hanegraaff exclaims, "the stakes of Christianity and culture in the controversy surrounding eschatology are enormous."[162] However, it seems Christians often shy away from eschatology for a few reasons: (1) they have been raised on 'Left Behind' theology; (2) eschatology is controversial (feelings can get hurt); and (3) probably more to the point, eschatological issues seem highly complex.

What I think it all comes down to is, Christians who are raised hearing rapture theology simply believe the church has always believed that way. *But what we have tried to make clear is 'Left Behind' eschatology is a work of fiction.* The sooner the church jettisons it, the better. We must therefore reject a seven-year period of tribulation on the basis that it is not found in Scripture. The reality that the Bible presents to us is quite different. In the pages of Holy Scripture, the saints are told to endure, hold fast, and persevere to the end while faithfully witnessing the gospel. And in these two concluding pages, our goal is to solidify that truth.

---

[162] Hank Hanegraaff, *The Apocalypse Code* (Nashville, TN: Thomas Nelson, 2007), xviii.

The Persecution and
Patient Endurance of the Saints

What we have tried to make abundantly clear is, God is not trying to defend Himself from the fact that He has apurpose for the church in tribulation. And despite tribulation, the church will endure; "For this light momentary affliction is preparing for us an eternal weight of glory beyond all comparison" (2 Cor 4:17). This eternal weight of glory is no doubt the glory of God in the salvation of all the elect. This is why the church endures all things (2 Tim 2:10). The church must continue to endure tribulation, in the power that God supplies, until Christ has gathered all His own out of the world (Jn 6:37). And finishing the Great Commission is going to cost some of us our lives, as it already has, and which it always has.

What Christ promises is spiritual protection through trials, not exemption from trials, for there is no promise in Scripture that God's people shall escape suffering and death, but there is the promise that no harm can come to our souls (Lk 21:18-19). God never promises the church deliverance *from* death, but deliverance *out of* death (Rev 20:6). *But the truly amazing thing is God employs our sufferings for His glory.* As C.S. Lewis puts it, "The sacrifice of Christ is repeated, or re-echoed, among His followers in varying degrees, from the cruelest martyrdom down to a self-submission of intention."[163] As has been said, the tribulation of the saints is therefore understood to be

---

[163] C. S. Lewis, *The Problem of Pain* (New York: MacMillan, 1962), 104.

the protracted death of Jesus Christ (2 Cor 4:10-11; Col 1:24).

What I hope has been abundantly clear is one's eschatology drives, or at least affects in large measure, one's evangelical beliefs and efforts. As has been argued, the rapture theory should be jettisoned from the teaching of the church, as such eschatology leaves God's people unprepared for trials and, for the most part, socially irresponsible. *The church must remain in the world until the end for the simple fact that the church is God's instrument for reaching the lost with the gospel* (Mt 28:20).

We learn endurance in the school of holy experience. The cross before the crown. The glory outstrips the sufferings. A witnessing church will always be a persecuted church. Christians will patiently-endure suffering, through the power God supplies, in order to fulfill the Great Commission and hasten the second coming of Christ (Mt 24:9-14). And in spite of tribulation in all its forms, love labors long and guides the work of faith, enabling believers, as mediating priests, to be self-squanders in Christ's service, seeking the recovery of the lost (Jn 11:52; 2 Tim 2:10).

Christ enlarges our hearts to include others, and enables His own to endure while the full number of God's people come in; for which the church is in labor (Is 26:17-19; 54:1-8; Jn 16:20-22; Rom 8:22-25; Gal 4:26-27; Rev 12:13-17); and these are the pangs of birth not death.

Endless Sabbath – Eternal Rest

In boundless age His Eternal decreed
Foreordained works His body dressed:
Quickening birth in His rising
Endless Sabbath – eternal rest.

Apollyon's brood light's countenance withheld
Er fleeting, nr seeing, nr wise:
Confused agitation twice death
Consigned oblivion – pride's demise.

From God-hewn Rock the kingdom upward grows
Course timed faith's reckoned innocence:
Never tasting death's damned sting
Played out course – divine providence.

From First Born of death all brethren numbered
Elect's surety, purchase effected:
At week's ending history's ceasing
Body redeemed – same body perfected.

God's breath and Spirit instantly gathered
His covered, hidden from wrath's might:
Patient endure their soul's possessed
Fullness of time – the Day's full light.

Fallen men and angels ante thronum [164]
Abraham's seed acquitted joyous:
Death's defeat impious to doom
Extra Ecclesium – nulla salus.[165]

Chosen broken vessels haply extol
Effectually drawn, winnowed, and blessed:
At length God's golden City descends
Endless Sabbath – eternal rest.

---

[164] Latin for 'before the throne.'
[165] Outside the Church there is no salvation.

Appendix 1:
Daniel's 70 Weeks

We have labored to demonstrate that God has a plan for tribulation and that His plan is for the church to not only live through all tribulation, including the Great Tribulation, but conquer through it. The purpose of this appendix to the book is to further discuss Daniel's 70th Week and its relevancy to our topic.

In the Book of Daniel, the prophet has been pondering about and praying about God's Jerusalem and the temple and the seventy years, but Gabriel enlightens Daniel to the fact that there are other seventies in God's program for Jerusalem. Seventies Daniel has not considered. This passage is one of the most difficult in the whole Bible. Moreover, interpretations have been legion.[166] H. C. Leupold observes: "Some interpreters despair completely of arriving at any certainty in their exposition, being overawed by the multiplicity of existing interpretations." However, with sober exegesis, we may arrive at an accurate interpretation.

Gabriel reveals to Daniel what will happen to Jerusalem in seventy periods of seven from the present time (about 539 BC). Daniel 9:20-27 declares:

> 20 Now while I was speaking, praying, and confessing my sin and the sin of my people Israel,

---

[166] Edward J. Young, *The Prophecy of Daniel* (Grand Rapids: Eerdmans, 1949), 191.

and presenting my supplication before the Lord my God for the holy mountain of my God, 21 yes, while I was speaking in prayer, the man Gabriel, whom I had seen in the vision at the beginning, being caused to fly swiftly, reached me about the time of the evening offering. 22 And he informed me, and talked with me, and said, "O Daniel, I have now come forth to give you skill to understand. 23 At the beginning of your supplications the command went out, and I have come to tell you, for you are greatly beloved; therefore consider the matter, and understand the vision: 24 "Seventy weeks are determined For your people and for your holy city, to finish the transgression, to make an end of sins, to make reconciliation for iniquity, to bring in everlasting righteousness, to seal up vision and prophecy, and to anoint the Most Holy. 25 "Know therefore and understand, that from the going forth of the command to restore and build Jerusalem until Messiah the Prince, there shall be seven weeks and sixty-two weeks; the street shall be built again, and the wall, even in troublesome times. 26 "And after the sixty-two weeks Messiah shall be cut off, but not for Himself; and the people of the prince who is to come shall destroy the city and the sanctuary. The end of it shall be with a flood, and till the end of the war desolations are determined. 27 Then he shall confirm a covenant with many for one week; but in the middle of the week He shall bring an end to sacrifice and offering. And on the wing of abominations shall be one who makes desolate, even until the consummation, which is determined, is poured out on the desolate.

There are several biblical truths we may note about this passage of Scripture:

1. The prophecy is an answer to Daniel's concern for the covenant.
2. This prophecy deals exclusively with the covenant and its fulfillment.
3. God's plan is bigger than the temple and goes beyond it. (God's answer of Daniel's prayer demonstrates that the real need of God's people is not merely a restored temple and city but eternal righteousness).
4. God says through the angel Gabriel that all of this will be accomplished by the Messiah.
5. God not only addresses Daniel's immediate concerns but shows him well off into the future how the covenant will be forever affected.

As Edward J. Young observes: "This is a divine revelation of the fact that a definite period of time has been decreed for the accomplishment of all that which is necessary for the true restoration of God's people from bondage."[167] It is safe to say that a week is seven years of duration, which means that the seventy weeks refers to 490 years. This period of time has been decreed by God for the accomplishment of His redemptive purposes.[168]

Beginning with verse 24, we may note that six things are to be accomplished within the seventy periods of seven. "Seventy weeks are determined for your people and for your holy city:

1. "To finish the transgression..." This carries a sense of fullness of sins, as in Genesis 15:16 where it is said the wicked cast themselves out by their own wickedness:

---

[167] Young, *The Prophecy of Daniel*, 195.
[168] Ibid, 197.

"For the iniquity of the Amorites is not yet complete" (cf. Dan 8:23). Israel's great sin was their rejection of the Messiah. As a result they were judicially condemned and hardened, their city and religious economy destroyed, and the people scattered all over the world (Lev 26:25-39; Luke 19:41-44).

The more graciously God waits for men, if, at length, instead of repenting they remain obstinate, the more severely does He avenge such great ingratitude.[169]

2. "To make an end of sins (to set a seal on sins)..." This was accomplished when Christ did away with sin with the sacrifice of Himself (Heb 9:26). Only in Jesus Christ has there ever been any such thing as the absolute forgiveness of sins. This line alone makes it certain that Christ's coming is here foretold.

3. "To make reconciliation for iniquity..." (To atone for wickedness). Literally, to set a seal σφραγίσαι on sins. This means to pardon, to blot out by means of a sin-offering, to forgive (Rom 5:8-10   ; Col 1:10). Here is a certain reference to the atonement for sins accomplished by Jesus Christ on Calvary, as a result of which "reconciliation of men to God" could occur. This is precisely the thing that restored the broken fellowship between man and God. To make an atonement is the technical word used fifty times in Leviticus for the offering of atoning sacrifice.

4. "To bring in everlasting righteousness..." Righteousness is right standing with God. Christ is indeed the source of righteousness. There cannot

---

[169] Calvin, Commentary on Genesis 15:16.

possibly be any other source of it. And He is the believer's righteousness (2 Cor 5:21).

5. "To seal up vision and prophecy..." (to set a signature as it were on the vision and prophecy which guarantees the promise (contents) of what was sealed – Heb 1:1). In other words, to confirm the ancient prophecies by a marvelous fulfillment in the ministry of Jesus Christ. Over 300 prophecies of the Old Testament pointing to the coming of Jesus Christ were fulfilled in His life, death, resurrection, and intercession.

6. "To anoint the most holy." Because of the absence of the article, as H.C. Leupold rightly observes, the Most Holy should "be rendered a Most Holy One."[170] This undoubtedly refers to the Messiah, the Most Holy One (cf. Ps 45:7 and Luke 4:18).

As Gleason Archer rightly observes: "The culmination of appointed years will witness the conclusion of man's 'transgression' or 'rebellion' against God - a development most naturally entered into with the establishment of an entirely new order on earth. This seems to require nothing less than the inauguration of the kingdom of God on earth." In other words, these six things therefore pertain not to the times of Antiochus, nor the second advent, but exclusively to the times of the first advent of Jesus Christ and the inauguration of His eternal kingdom. "The time is fulfilled, and the kingdom of God is at hand. Repent and believe the gospel "(Mk 1:15).

---

[170] H. C. Leupold, *Exposition of Daniel* (Grand Rapids: Baker, 1969), 414.

The Three Divisions of the 70 Weeks

In Daniel 9:25-27 there are three periods of time. Verse 25 mentions two of them and verse 27 mentions the third. The first period is seven sevens long. The second period is be sixty-two sevens long. And the third period is be one seven long. Daniel 9:25 goes on to advance the prophecy by giving the *terminus a quem* for the seventy weeks, namely from the date of the commandment to restore and to rebuild the city of Jerusalem. Here Gabriel reveals to Daniel the starting point for the seventy-weeks prophecy. There was a command to restore and build Jerusalem in history that began this specific time period. This was somewhat subsequent to the end of the Babylonian captivity in 539 BC.

The difficulty is compounded by our ignorance of just exactly when this commandment went forth. The Bible presents four possible decrees that might fulfill this description: (1) the decree of Cyrus – this gave Ezra and the Babylonian captives the right to return to Jerusalem and rebuild the temple in 538 BC (Ezra 1:1-4 and Ezra 5:13-17); (2) the decree of Darius – this gave Ezra the right to continue to rebuild the temple in 517 BC (Ezra 6:6-12); (3) the decree of Artaxerxes – this gave Ezra permission, safe passage, and supplies to return to Jerusalem to rebuild the temple in 458 BC (Ezra 7:11-26); and (4) the decree of Artaxerxes – this gave Nehemiah permission, safe passage and supplies to return to Jerusalem to rebuild the city and the walls in 445 BC (Nehemiah 2:1-8).

The fourth decree, that of Artaxerxes, is the most likely candidate. ii. Only the last of these four decrees was a command to restore and build Jerusalem. For whereas the first three focus on the temple, only the fourth focuses on the street or on the wall (cf. Dan 9:25).

It is possible to miss the forest for the trees. But by our best calculations, 490 days being equal to 490 years, we may understand verse 25 to equate as follows: 445BC + 483 years (69 weeks) = 32 AD (prophetic years of 360 days each year) = 173,880 days. Thus, "from the going forth of the command (of Artaxerxes in 445 BC) to restore and build Jerusalem (Neh 2:1-8) until Messiah the Prince, there shall be seven weeks and sixty-two weeks (483 years); the street shall be built again, and the wall, even in troublesome times (Nehemiah 1:3). "Until Messiah the Prince" most likely refers to Christ's triumphal entry. Fulfilling the prophecy to the day (483 years later), Jesus presented Himself as Messiah the Prince to Israel.

Next, as verse 26 declares, two events are to occur: (1) the cutting off of the Messiah; and (2) the destruction of the city. As Edward J. Young makes clear, "This verse does not state how long after the 62 sevens these things will take place but from verse 27 we learn that the cutting off of the anointed One occurs in the middle of the 70th seven."[171] The words "cut off" in this verse refer to Christ's crucifixion and death on the cross at Calvary (Is 53:8, 12).

In consequence for the cutting off of the Messiah, the people of a coming prince will destroy the city and sanctuary (temple).[172]   Again, interpretations are

---

[171] Young, *The Prophecy of Daniel*, 206.
[172] Ibid, 206.

legion, but it seems most likely that these people are the Romans, and the coming prince is the Roman general, and later emperor, Titus. The further references to the destruction of Jerusalem, "the flood," and "the war," etc. are prophecies of the great tribulations that should overwhelm Jerusalem at the times when her doom was executed by the armies of Vespasian and Titus in the year 70 AD. They were in fact the instrument of God's wrath (Luke 19:41-44). After all, the city and the sanctuary are said to be destroyed, not by a prince, but by the people of that prince.[173] Further, the destruction of Jerusalem was itself a type of judgment that befalls the city of man (Is 26).

The final seven comes in verse 27. This verse is the crux of the whole 70 weeks of years. One's interpretation of it therefore determines the overall meaning of the prophecy. The first part of verse 27 declares: "Then he shall **confirm a covenant** with many for one week; but in the middle of the week He shall bring an end to sacrifice and offering."

Many have taken this to refer to a future covenant the nation of Israel will make with the Antichrist as a political messiah. However, I would suggest to you that this does not refer to the Antichrist at all but to Jesus Christ who makes a covenant that will prevail with His people. So what we have is a description of a covenant with many that is *gabar* strengthened and will thus prevail. As Edward J. Young demonstrates:

> It is a mistake to say that these words speak of the making of a seven-year covenant, and to infer that

---

[173] Ibid, 208.

the maker of it cannot be the Messiah whose covenant is an everlasting covenant. The reference, therefore, is not to the making of a covenant but to a covenant which has already been made.[174]

The point is: Christ fulfilled the covenant by confirming and strengthening it (Is 42:6; 52:13-53:12; Dan 9:27; cf. Heb 8:6; 9:16-28).

The second part of the verse declares, "He shall bring an end to sacrifice and offering." I would suggest to you that soteriologically this happened when Jesus finished a perfect atonement for sins on the cross, and historically it happened when the temple was destroyed. This is why Heb 8:13 says, when Jesus made "A new covenant," He has made the first obsolete. And this was fulfilled "in the middle of the week," that is after three and one half years of Christ's earthly ministry (26-30 AD).

Then we are told "And on the wing of abominations shall be one who makes *desolate*, even until the consummation, which is determined, is poured out on the desolate" (9:27b). In other words, within the temple will be an abomination which causes desolation. What we should see here is, after Christ's finished atonement on the cross, sacrifices were continued to be offered in the temple for about 40 years. These were completely worthless and abominable. Jesus saw Himself as the replacement of the Temple (Jn 2:19-22). Jesus said, "See! Your house is left to you *desolate*" (Mt 23:38). Christ indeed condemned the city to total destruction, a prophecy actually fulfilled nearly forty years after Christ spoke

---

[174] Ibid, 209.

the imprecation of Luke 19:41-44. I would suggest that this refers to the destruction of the temple because of the desolating abominations as Jesus declares in Luke 21:20: "But when you see Jerusalem surrounded by armies, then know that its desolation is near." And so in AD 70, when the temple is destroyed the sacrifices are no longer able to be made. This understanding of Daniel's 70 weeks is most in line with the ECFs and the older orthodox.

The point is: When we lose sight of the new covenant we become lost. This is a prophecy of the Messiah's atoning death to once for all bring in the blessings of the new covenant and do away with the old. As Heb 8:13 says, by making and confirming and strengthening "A new covenant," He has made the first obsolete. This is also a prediction of the destruction of the temple which is very significant in light of the finished and completed work of Jesus Christ. Thus, the destruction of Jerusalem is here plainly included within the seventy weeks. So what is in view here is the inauguration of the new covenant and the end of the old covenant.

One question remains: What about the other half of the 70th week? It seems the 70th week represents what has happened since Jesus Christ's first advent and what will continue until His second advent. Interestingly, the time span of half a week of years is 42 months, 1,260 days, and 3 ½ years – enormously important time periods in the Book of Revelation, mentioned seven times (Rev 11:2, 3, 9, 11; 12:6, 14; 13:5).

I would suggest to you that this duration of time signifies the period of time between Christ's ascension and second coming. This is also the duration between

Christ's inauguration and consummation of His kingdom, as well as the testing of believers, and the predominance of evil (Dan 7:25; 12:7).[175] The 70th 'seven' will continue till the return of Jesus Christ.

All of this is important for a number of reasons: The prophecy of Daniel 9 is all about a restoration that is completed by the long-awaited Messiah – Jesus Christ. We have an accomplished redemption in Jesus Christ. Christ is the true temple of which we are a part. Christ has already done for us everything the temple was supposed to do. The only thing we are waiting for is the return of the King.

In Daniel's time the people of God's priorities had been off. They had made the outward means of their religion the priority and the heart of their existence the very heart of worship a secondary matter. And for this as we know they were carried away into captivity. They had to have their priorities corrected. They had 70 years to think about that. And after 70 years, God moved the heart of the pagan king Cyrus to bring them back to the land (Ezra 1:1). And the people come back to the land and rebuilt the temple. Later, God moved the heart of Artaxerxes to give the command to rebuild the city and its walls.

When God's people came back and rebuild the temple and city, by doing so they were preparing the way of the Lord, making ready the stage on which the great Kingdom of God drama of the future would be enacted. For it was to Jerusalem and to the temple that our Lord Jesus Himself eventually did come to

---

[175] The 1,260 days, 42 months and 3 ½ years corresponds to the 42 encampments during the wilderness wanderings of the Hebrews before reaching the Promised Land. These are recorded in Numbers 33:1-39.

announce that the Kingdom had drawn near in His Person and work (Mal 3:1). As the NT declares, He is the true temple for which the former temple pointed the way. The temple our spiritual ancestors were building all points the true temple of Christ's body which you and I are a part of by faith (1 Pet 2:4-9).

"He shall strengthen the covenant with many" (Dan 9:27).

Appendix 2:
Creeds of Christendom

"The Bible is the Word of God to man; the Creed is man's answer to God." – Philip Schaff

The Apostle's Creed [176]

I believe in God, the Father Almighty, the Creator of heaven and earth, and in Jesus Christ, His only Son, our Lord: Who was conceived of the Holy Spirit, born of the Virgin Mary, suffered under Pontius Pilate, was crucified, died, and was buried.

He descended into hell. [1] The third day He arose again from the dead. He ascended into heaven and sits at the right hand of God the Father Almighty, whence He shall come to judge the living and the dead. I believe in the Holy Spirit, the holy catholic [2] church, the communion of saints, the forgiveness of sins, the resurrection of the body, and life everlasting. Amen.

End Notes:

1. "Descended into hell" does not refer to literally going down into the bowels of hell itself to be subject to the devil. Rather, it is a poetic way of stating that

---

[176] The Apostles' Creed was not written by the Biblical Disciples. The name is deemed this as a sum and substance of the early Apostolic teaching which the disciples would have held to. Earliest version found is A.D. 215. The current version is circa 542 A.D.

Christ truly and assuredly died on the cross, and His body remained under the power of death for three days.

2. The word "catholic" refers not to the Roman Catholic Church, but to the universal church of the Lord Jesus Christ. Catholic *katholikos* means universal in Greek.

The Nicene Creed
381 A.D. [177]

I believe in one God, the Father Almighty, maker of heaven and earth, and of all things visible and invisible; And in one Lord Jesus Christ, the only begotten Son of God, begotten of his Father before all worlds, God of God, Light of Light, very God of very God, begotten, not made, being of one substance with the Father; by whom all things were made; who for us men and for our salvation came down from heaven, and was incarnate by the Holy Ghost of the Virgin Mary, and was made man; and was crucified also for us under Pontius Pilate; he suffered and was buried; and the third day he rose again according to the Scriptures, and ascended into heaven, and sitteth on the right hand of the Father; and he shall come again, with glory, to judge both the quick and the dead; whose kingdom shall have no end.

And I believe in the Holy Ghost, the Lord, and Giver of Life, who proceedeth from the Father and the Son; who with the Father and the Son together is worshipped and glorified; who spake by the Prophets. And I believe one holy Catholic and Apostolic Church; I acknowledge one baptism for the remission of sins; and I look for the resurrection of the dead, and the life of the world to come. Amen.

End Notes:

---

[177] In its present form it is the Creed of the whole Christian Church, the Greek Church (Orthodox) rejecting only the last added clause. A. A. Hodge, A Short History of Creeds and Confessions, 4

1. The Nicene Creed is formed on the basis of the Apostles' Creed. The clauses relating to the consubstantial divinity of Christ were contributed by the great Council held in Nicaea in A.D. 325; those relating to the divinity and personality of the Holy Ghost added by the Second Ecumenical Council, held at Constantinople in A.D.381.

2. The filioque clause, "and the Son," was added by the Council of the Western Church held at Toledo, Spain in A.D. 569.

The Definition of Chalcedon [178]
Oct 22, 451 AD

We, then, following the holy Fathers, all with one consent, teach men to confess one and the same Son, our Lord Jesus Christ, the same perfect in Godhead and also perfect in manhood; truly God and truly man, of a reasonable [rational] soul and body; consubstantial [coessential] with the Father according to the Godhead, and consubstantial with us according to the Manhood; in all things like unto us, without sin; begotten before all ages of the Father according to the Godhead, and in these latter days, for us and for our salvation, born of the Virgin Mary, the Mother of God, according to the Manhood; one and the same Christ, Son, Lord, **Only-begotten,** to be acknowledged in two natures, *inconfusedly,   unchangeably, indivisibly, inseparably;* the distinction of natures being by no means taken away by the union, but rather the property of each nature being preserved, and concurring in one Person and one Subsistence, not parted or divided into two persons, but one and the same Son, and only begotten, God the Word, the Lord Jesus Christ, as the prophets from the beginning [have declared] concerning him, and the Lord Jesus Christ himself has taught us, and the Creed of the holy Fathers has handed down to us.

---

[178] The Chalcedonian Definition, repudiated the notion of a single nature in Christ, and declared that He has two natures in one person and hypostasis; it also insists on the completeness of his two natures: Godhead and manhood.

Bibliography

Primary Sources

Augustine. *The City of God*. Marcus Dods, Translator. New York: Modern Library, 1993.

Bettenson, Henry S. *The Early Christian Fathers*. Oxford: Oxford University Press, 1956.

Chrysostom, John. *Homilies on Colossians*. Oxford: James Parker, 1879.

Davies, Philip R. *IQM, the War Scroll from Qumran: Its Structure and History*. Rome: Biblical Institute Press, 1977.

Eusebius Pamphilus. *The Ecclesiastical History*. Isaac Boyle, Editor. Christian Frederick Cruse, Translator. Grand Rapids: Baker, 1993.

Hoole, Charles H. *The Shepherd of Hermas*. Charles H. Hoole, Translator. Oxford: Rivingtons, 1870.

Justin Martyr. *The First and Second Apologies*. Leslie William Barnard, Translator. Mahwah: Paulist Press, 1997.

Quasten, Johannes, and James A. Kleist. *The Didache: The Epistle of Barnabus, the Epistles and the Martyrdom of St. Polycarp, the Fragments of Papias, the Epistle to Diognetus*. Mahwah, NJ: Paulist Press, 1948.

Roberts, Alexander, ed. *The Ante-Nicene Fathers: The Writings of the Fathers Down to AD 325 Volume I-the Apostolic Fathers with Justin Martyr and Irenaeus*. Cosimo, Inc., 2007.

Shelton, Brian W. *Martyrdom from Exegesis in Hippolytus: An Early Church Presbyter's Commentary on Daniel*. Eugene, OR: Wipf and Stock, 2008.

Sibbes, Richard. *The Complete Works of Richard Sibbes. Vol. 3*. Edinburgh: James Nichol, 1862.

Tertullian. *Apology and De Spectaculis*. Harvard: Harvard University Press, 1931.

Secondary Sources

Beale, Gregory. K. *The Book of Revelation: The New International Greek Testament Commentary*. Grand Rapids: Eerdmans, 1999.

——— *New Testament Biblical Theology: The Unfolding of the Old Testament in the New*. Grand Rapids: Baker, 2011.

Cara, Robert J. *A Study Commentary on 1 and 2 Thessalonians*. Darlington: Evangelical Press, 2009.

Carson, Donald A. *Love in Hard Places*. Wheaton, IL: Crossway, 2002.

Chafer, Lewis Sperry, and John F. Walvoord. *Major Bible Themes*. Grand Rapids: Zondervan, 1974.

Clowney, Edmund P. *The Message of 1 Peter*. Downers Grove: InterVarsity Press, 1989.

Daley, Brian E. *The Hope of the Early Church: A Handbook of Patristic Eschatology*. Grand Rapids: Baker, 1991.

DeMar, Gary. *Last Days Madness: Obsession of the Modern Church.* Powder Springs: American Vision Press, 1999.

Frend, W.W. *Martyrdom and Persecution in the Early Church: A Study of Conflict from the Maccabees to Donatus.* Eugene, OR: Wipf and Stock, 2014.

Gerstner, John H. *Wrongly Dividing the Word of Truth: A Critique of Dispensationalism.* Grand Rapids: Soli Deo Gloria, 2007.

Gundry, Robert. *The Church and the Tribulation.* Grand Rapids: Zondervan, 1973.

Hill, Charles E. *Regnum Caelorum: Patterns of Millennial Thought in Early Christianity.* Grand Rapids: Eerdmans, 2001.

Hodge, Charles. *Commentary on the Second Epistle to the Corinthians.* Grand Rapids: Eerdmans, 1950.

Ice, Thomas, and Timothy J. Demy, eds. *The Return: Understanding Christ's Second Coming and the End Times.* Grand Rapids: Kregel, 1999.

Ladd, George E. *The Blessed Hope.* Grand Rapids: Eerdmans, 1956.

LaHaye, Tim. *No Fear of the Storm: Why Christians Will Escape All the Tribulation* (Sisters, OR: Multnomah, 1992.

Motyer, Alec J. *The Prophecy of Isaiah: An Introduction and Commentary.* Downers Grove: IVP, 1993.

Murray, Iain Hamish. *The Puritan Hope: Revival and the Interpretation of Prophecy.* Carlisle: Banner of Truth, 1971.

Pitre, Brant James. *Jesus, the Tribulation, and the End of the Exile: Restoration Eschatology and the Origin of the Atonement*. Grand Rapids: Baker, 2005.

Scofield, Cyrus I. *The Scofield Reference Bible: The Holy Bible, Containing the Old and New Testaments*. Oxford: Oxford University Press, 1917.

Related Articles

Bauckham, Richard J., "The Great Tribulation in the Shepherd of Hermas." The Journal of Theological Studies (1974): 27-40.

Brown, Schuyler. "The Hour of Trial"(Rev 3: 10)." Journal of Biblical Literature 85, no. 3 (1966): 308-314.

DeSilva, David A. "The Social Setting of the Revelation to John: Conflicts Within, Fears Without." Westminster Theological Journal 54 (1992): 273-302.

Gustafson, Henry. "The Afflictions of Christ: What is Lacking?." BR 8 (1963): 28-42.

Lea, Thomas D. "A Survey of the Doctrine of the Return of Christ in the Ante-Nicene Fathers," Journal of the Evangelical Theological Society 29, no. 2 (1986): 169.

Kline, Meredith G. "The Covenant of the Seventieth Week." The Law and the Prophets: Old Testament Studies in Honor of Oswald T. Allis (1974): 452-469.

Mattill, Andrew J. "The Way of Tribulation." Journal of Biblical Literature 98, no. 4 (1979): 531-546.

Russell, Walt, III. "Do We Need to Evangelize All Peoples Before Christ Returns?" Mission Frontiers 16:7-8, 1994.

Scripture Index

Scripture Index

Scripture Index

Scripture Index

Scripture Index

Paul D. LeFavor was born in Virginia and educated at Liberty University, and Reformed Theological Seminary. He is a service-disabled, retired US Army Special Forces Master Sergeant, who is married to Becky, his wife of twenty-two years, and has two daughters Liane and Collette. He currently serves as the pastor of Christ Covenant Baptist Church in Fayetteville, North Carolina.

Among his published works are *The US Army Small Unit Tactics Handbook, Iron Sharpening Iron* and *Tactical Leadership*.